CAST THE FIRST STONE

CAST THE FIRST STONE

ETHICS IN ANALYTIC PRACTICE

Edited and with an introduction by
Lena B. Ross and Manisha Roy

Foreword by Adolf Guggenbühl-Craig

CHIRON PUBLICATIONS • WILMETTE, ILLINOIS

© 1995 by Chiron Publications. All rights reserved. No part of this publication may be reproduced, stored in a retrieval system, or transmitted, in any form by any means, electronic, mechanical, photocopying or otherwise, without the prior written permission of the publisher, Chiron Publications, 400 Linden Avenue, Wilmette, Illinois 60091. (708) 256–7551.

Library of Congress Catalog Card Number: 94–40573

Printed in the United States of America.
Copyediting and book design by Siobhan Drummond.
Cover design by D. J. Hyde.

Library of Congress Cataloging-in-Publication Data:

Cast the first stone : ethics in analytic practice / edited and with an introduction
    by Lena B. Ross and Manisha Roy : foreword by Adolf Guggenbühl-Craig.
        p. cm.
    Includes bibliographical references.
    ISBN 0–933029–89–6
    1. Sex between psychotherapist and patient—Moral and ethical aspects. 2.
Psychoanalysis—Moral and ethical aspects. I. Ross, Lena B., 1951–   . II. Roy,
Manisha, 1936–   .
    RC489.S47C37   1995
    174′.2—dc20
                                                        94–40573
                                                                     CIP

    ISBN 0–933029–89–6

CONTENTS

Part IV   BEHIND ETHICS: ARCHETYPAL DIMENSIONS

FOREWORD

Although *Cast the First Stone* is a book that looks at the psychology of ethics generally, the ethical violation of sexual acting out holds a particularly central place. Of the possible ethical transgressions, this causes the most damage and provokes the most heated discussion. Yet to write about the problem of sexual acting out during psychotherapy and analysis presumably should be very simple. One just has to stay within the correct psychological and political images. Discussions of sexual acting out can only exist within this context, and with the understanding that the following statements must always be respected because they are correct.

Any kind of sexual acting out during psychotherapy has to be condemned; every acting out during therapy harms the patient psychologically. Sexual acting out during therapy is so harmful because it is a misuse of a power position within a transference. It misuses the trust of the patient and is psychologically experienced as incest; therefore, the responsibility for any kind of sexual acting out lies completely with the therapist.

Sexual transgressions in analysis have to be dealt with very severely and, whenever they become known, have to be brought to the attention of professional committees, medical or psychological authorities, etc. The culprit must abstain from practicing therapy for several years and has to undergo further analysis.

This being understood, why publish a book in which the problems of sexual transgression in analysis and psychotherapy figure prominently, although the topic is ethics generally? One could perhaps investigate further why some analysts are so unprofessional or so criminal as to indulge in these transgressions; but the evaluation of the transgression is made and stands firm.

There is, however, one aspect of this theme which complicates the matter. We all agree that from an ethical point of view every therapist has the obligation to do the patient every possible good. The first rule of medical and therapeutic practice is *primum nil nocere* ("first of all, do no harm"). There is no one among the psychological or medical profession who can claim that one is justified in harming the patient, and acting out sexually is one of the major ways of inflicting such harm.

However, we are under an obligation to find out what does harm the patient and what helps. In that way, we can take nothing for granted, nothing is certain. It is our sacred duty to investigate continually how a patient can be helped and how harm can be avoided. In some way, we have to question over and over again what we are doing and what we believe.

Here, a certain dogmatism in the psychologically correct attitude towards sexual transgression in psychotherapy becomes damaging. It hinders serious research, serious questioning of what we are doing, and makes us incapable of assessing our actions and theories.

This dogmatism leads very often to strange results. The correct psychological attitude insists, for instance, that the patient is never responsible for any kind of sexual acting out. If a patient and analyst decide to finish therapy and to begin an erotic relationship, it is still unprofessional and unethical, because even in this decision, the patient is the victim of the power of the analyst, of the power of the transference. Even if there is a great deal of truth in this, don't we, by having this attitude, again commit some transgression in the psychological, ethical, and political field? We declare that a human being, a patient, an adult citizen, is an irresponsible abused child. We take away from him or her the possibility of making certain decisions. Is this not a devaluation of the human dignity of the adult patient?

Perhaps a belief in the magical power of psychotherapy lies behind this attitude. Once in psychotherapy, a magical spell has been cast over the patient. Even years after analysis, decisions concerning his or her relationship to the analyst are not valid, not respected. I myself firmly believe that any kind of sexual acting out during therapy is damaging. But my beliefs are not relevant here. As a psychologist and psychiatrist, I have to question over and over the foundation of my work. Even if I am quite sure about something, I still have to realize that there is hardly any certainty in psychology or medicine, or in any human knowledge. Until the sixteenth century, humanity was quite sure that the sun revolved around the earth, and yet this secure knowledge and belief turned out to be an error.

A medical professor of mine, Wilhelm Löffler, never talked about present medical knowledge but only about "the present stage of medical error." This desirable open attitude towards anything we do medically and psychologically can be deeply hampered by dogmatic beliefs. We have to act according to guidelines, but at the same time, we always have to question our basic assumptions.

Concerning sexual transgressions in psychotherapy, this is not easy, because a dogmatism has taken over which has almost religious dimensions. Anybody who questions the basic assumption is automatically a criminal or a nonprofessional, a charlatan. Because of the dangers of dogmatism, I think it is important to publish a book in which these problems have a major focus, one to which *many* authors have contributed. To dare one author to question all of the assumptions in this or any area of ethics would be asking too much. He or she would be immediately ostracized by the well-meaning but dogmatic professional community, particularly when exploring the question of sexual acting out. With many authors, each need only concentrate on some of the aspects of the dogma.

I want, however, to avoid misunderstanding. It could be that when we question the basic assumptions of our attitudes towards sexual transgressions in analysis or psychotherapy, we come to the same conclusion as before. That something has become a dogma does not mean that it is false, but simply that we are not allowed to speculate about it anymore—it has become a "fact." I think every responsible therapist, psychologist, and doctor tries to keep to the rules and regulations currently established and commonly believed to be right, those based on the present state of knowledge or error. A responsible analyst will, for example, never become involved sexually with patients, for the sake of both the analyst and the patient. However, there is much to be explored in this area of ethics.

One interesting part of the whole equation is the aspect of the contract. Every patient at the commencement of therapy makes a contract with the therapist, as does the therapist with the patient. The contract is not formulated in writing or in words. It is a so-called silent contract, which is legally problematic but morally binding. The common assumption is that the therapist does not get involved sexually with a patient. Therefore, the silent contract says that sexual involvement with patients is neither possible nor desirable. The therapist presents himself or herself to the patient as a man or woman who will not become sexually involved: *pacta servanda sunt,* contracts must be kept.

This does not imply, however, that we are forbidden to investigate whether the base of the contract is helpful to the patient or not. If a book like this gives psychologists and doctors courage to keep on searching for the "truth," it will have been worthwhile. That courage is needed, for even as I write, I fear that I will be misunderstood. In my opinion, it is certainly essential not to become involved sexually with a patient—on this question I myself have hardly any doubts. But we are obligated also to ask ourselves if our knowledge of the subject is accurate, is not a complete misunderstanding. Serious research has always shed more light on what seemed to be obvious. Einstein put the absolute nature of space and time into doubt. Dr. Ignaz Philipp Semmelweiss, the famous Hungarian obstetrician, saved the lives of thousands of women who gave birth to children in their "dirty" homes, which turned out to be safer than the apparently sanitized hospitals where the danger of infection was greater.

It would be interesting to investigate the question of why we are often inclined to make out of so-called scientific facts— whether psychological or physical—almost a religious dogma. This applies especially to our opinions about sexual life. In my youth, there were still physicians who claimed that if a girl had sexual intercourse before marriage, her character would be damaged forever and her joy of life greatly impaired. During the whole nineteenth century and into the twentieth century, medicine strongly asserted that masturbation was extremely damaging. Medical men thought they knew for sure that masturbation led to physical and psychological damage.

In medicine and psychotherapy, ethical behavior means one tries to do whatever seems to be the most useful and therapeutic action at the time, realizing that our knowledge is never absolutely sure. There is always room for new information and insight. Even more, it is our duty to question everything we are doing.

Adolf Guggenbühl-Craig

Adolf Guggenbühl-Craig, *M.D., is a Jungian analyst and psychiatrist in private practice in Zurich and a training analyst and lecturer at the C. G. Jung Institute of Zurich. He is an adviser for young criminals and former president of the International Association for Analytical Psychology (IAAP). He is the author of numerous articles and several books including* Power in the Helping Professions, Marriage Dead or Alive, Eros on Crutches, *and* From the Wrong Side.

INTRODUCTION

I

The idea for this book came out of a conversation which the editors had at the International Congress for Analytical Psychology in 1992. At the time, it seemed that everyone was talking about ethics in analytic practice, but always from the somewhat narrow perspective of who had been reported to have done what to whom and what, in a behavioral sense, should be done about it. It seemed to us that in the fury of the contemporary discourse, the one uniquely Jungian aspect was missing, that is, the symbolic attitude, which means inclusion of the mythological and psychological aspects of psyche. This is not to say that there was not fairly universal agreement on certain ethical principles, e.g., that the analyst must not sleep with the analysand. Rather, it seemed to us that beyond the concrete points obvious to all, no one was being allowed to look at material relating to ethics in the way that analytical psychologists look at all other material, i.e., to discern its multifaceted meanings.

We felt that a book dedicated to presenting varying viewpoints regarding the psychology of ethics might serve to stimulate dialogue about this seemingly contentious topic. We have called our book *Cast the First Stone*, and the title alone generated an intercontinental mini-storm long before the actual essays were even written. Many of those reacting had their own ideas about what the title must mean and why it had been chosen. Although thrown somewhat by the strong reactions to the title, our intuition that such a book was timely was confirmed, and our determination to stick with both the title and the topic was strengthened.

The title was chosen for more than one reason. Our intention was to try to get beyond the place where it seemed the dialogue was stuck, the place where only one action seemed to be sanctioned, that of casting stones, which can only end in a metaphorical death. Then there is the biblical allusion itself, the tale of the woman taken in adultery, which appears in the Gospel of John in the New Testament. In that tale, a woman is taken before Jesus and accused of committing adultery, for which the penalty was stoning. Her accusers hoped to trap Jesus by forcing him to judge her, thus denying his own teachings wherein redemption (transformation) is central rather than judgment and its concomitant punishment. Jesus, however, says nothing, but he writes with his finger in the sand; we are not told what, if anything, he writes. Eventually he says, "He that is without sin among you, let him first cast a stone at her," refusing to judge. This forces the men to think, and finally, one by one, they drift away. In our book, Plaut refers to the forgiveness inherent in such an act and speculates whether it is enough for contemporary times. Gordon also cites this passage, but treats it more as a lesson to us to reflect on these matters within ourselves.

There is, however, a third way of reading this biblical passage, one related to a thread which runs through other spiritual writings. Jesus is able, through his initial acts of writing cryptically on the ground and then asking a question, to insert a pause between the impulse and the action. He introduces reflection into the equation, instead of rules. Although rules are necessary codes for living, they are culturally based and so can outlive their usefulness to the development of psyche. One traditional method of shifting course has been through changing the direction of thought, discourse, and ultimately action. This theme can also be found in Koranic writings, where patience (*sabr*) is required in order to achieve revelation when a matter is not understood, as in the well-known tale of Moses and the Archangel Gabriel. The shift from pre-Islamic to Islamic times included a transition from the ethic of impulsiveness (*jahl*) to the virtues of reason (*hilm*); in this shift, impulsivity, which had been viewed as a heroic virtue, came to be seen as wrong and shameful. In fact, these various shifts from the impulsive to the reflective in monotheistic religion could be said to have their beginnings in Abraham's argument with Yahweh over the destruction of Sodom (Genesis 18:20–33). Yahweh initially vows the total destruction of everyone there, but in a long discussion over the righteous versus the wicked, Abraham manages to convince God to reflect, change his mind, and decide that anyone who is righteous will be allowed to live. Similar messages come from the ancient traditions of India. Indian religious texts often

speak of the paramount virtue of *vidya*, or knowledge, consciousness as opposed to *avidya*, or ignorance, in matters of ethics and
morality. In the *Bhagavad Gita* (part of the great epic
Mahābhārata), the further complications of this idea are illustrated
by the hero warrior Arjuna listening to the wise advice of his friend
and guide, the god Krishna.

Krishna's advice comes when knowledge fails to solve the
dilemma and action is inevitable. Arjuna must fight a devastating
battle against his evil cousins. Krishna helps Arjuna with his moral
and emotional dilemma by advising him not to worry about the
outcome, only to remain in the process. Ultimately the result of the
war between good and evil is irrelevant; no one really wins. Or,
rather, there is no virtue in winning (see Luigi Zoja's essay,
"Reflections Concerning Ethics"). Transcendence can happen only
when the battle is fought without concern for the results. Only
then can peace prevail until another dilemma arises and the next
cycle of process must be lived. (Some essays within this book,
notably those by Ulanov and Roy, focus on an appeal to serve Self
or psyche as a method of achieving resolution to the dilemmas of
ethics.) These and other stories from a variety of religious and folkloric sources highlight the function of reflection in the development of psyche. It is our hope that the essays here will contribute
to a reflective aspect which we feel has been missing in the current
debate over ethics.

II

Ethics evolve over time and from different sources. June Singer
opens the first section of the book, Evolution of Ethics, with her
essay, "Ethics at the Fountainhead," an intimate portrait of the
growth of an ethic which she had to develop over years. From her
training days in Zurich at the end of Jung's life through contemporary thoughts about how ethics develop and what they mean,
Singer starts our process of exploration with her story of coming to
understand the meaning of ethics for the analyst through personal
experiences, many of which were painful and bewildering. Anyone
who has trained as an analyst will recognize the kinds of ethical

dilemmas that can emerge for the candidate and must ultimately be resolved by the analyst.

Psychological issues regarding ethics have been around as long as analytical psychology; after all, they are only a subset of the larger issues that have always concerned humans once they are in groups. In 1949, Erich Neumann wrote *Depth Psychology and the New Ethic* in an attempt to outline a structure of the evolution of ethics in analytical psychology, as he saw it. In "Eros, Mutuality and the 'New Ethic,'" John Haule discusses Neumann's ideas and his own further resolution of the issue of the "tension between the demands of the collective and those of the Self." From our experience with this book, that tension appears to be one that, for many of our authors, presents perhaps the most difficult question. Do we see ourselves in service to the Self in all things and is this at odds with the demands of our society?

Haule's resolution, his further development of Neumann's original thesis, is the concept of mutuality: through an imaginal, painstaking examination of his own process as an analyst, Haule is able to come to a conclusion regarding mutuality as a synthesis of the concerns of ego and Self. In her essay, "The Need for an Analytic Temenos," Florence C. Irvine chronicles quite a different journey, in the sense that it involves an entire community. The San Francisco Jungians passed ten painful and tumultuous years of changing attitudes, and in her essay Irvine documents that long road, at the end of which consensus was reached that the temenos of the patient was, after all, the most important factor. It is possible to see, from Irvine's careful analysis of the violence that can occur to a patient's psyche with the failure to establish a safe container for the work, how this conclusion was reached.

In our next section, Metatheories of Ethics, we leave the realm of evolving ethics and turn to a discussion of what might be called structural ethos. While ethics is about the moral relationship of the individual to the community, ethos is about fundamental values of cultures. These two topics are related, as they share a common Greek root. Nevertheless, the emphasis differs. In the first essay, "The Scheherazade Solution: Power Abuse and an Ethic of Transformation," Lena B. Ross highlights the nature of power abuses that have emerged within our rigid ethical system, perhaps because our system emerged from a single type of consciousness and is in need of the balancing of another type of awareness for completeness. She also emphasizes the appearance, early in our history and just at the time of a consolidation of masculine consciousness, of a compensatory phenomenon in the form of fiction: new to the literary stage, this innovative form speaks with a different voice, tells an alternate tale, and offers a far different method of resolution, that is, the *transformation* of energy which can be reabsorbed back into the community as useful rather than excised as destructive. To illustrate her point, Ross has used an ancient Arabic tale compensatory to the development of Middle Eastern consciousness as we know it today.

Henry Hanoch Abramovitch, in a compelling discussion that sets up an analogy between Jewish tradition and analytical psychology, offers another viewpoint from the Middle East, in which the traditions of Jewish culture can be seen as oscillating between prophetic and legalistic modes. Abramovitch argues that both are needed and, together, tend to form a cycle. That is, at times, the voice of the Self, or God, comes through powerfully, and then the individual is compelled to follow it at all cost. At other times, however, the health of the community must come first, and this is the more usual basis for Jewish life. (Perhaps it is the legalistic mode that preserves the community, while the prophetic mode allows it to change and evolve.) There is a clear sense in Abramovitch's essay that the two modes alternate and that both are necessary.

In "Reflections Concerning Ethics," Luigi Zoja begins with the consideration mentioned earlier: that ethics of analysis must be understood in the context of a general system of ethics, and that since ethics come out of culture, as cultures differ, so will the understanding of ethics. He then proceeds to discuss the many threads that have gone into ethics in Western life, to question some of the bases of the early origins, and to make a distinction between *de facto* ethics and *de jure,* that is, thought that came about as a result of concrete actions versus ethics that emerged as a matter of right. He uses this distinction first to discuss ethics which derive from the outcome of actions (*de facto*), then to a kind of Darwinian derivative of the "survival of the fittest," which Zoja calls the "ethics of the winner," while holding out himself for ethics that derive from natural rights (*de jure*). He points out the necessity for

ethics which will look for justice, not merely the condemnation of
those whom we feel are aberrant from our codes.

Moving on from this general discussion of an ethical framework, Zoja turns to a more detailed study of the ethics of conviction versus responsibilities, arriving at a more personally compelling focus on the effects of any attempt to codify transactions
between analyst and analysand minutely and what this does to the
transference. He focuses next on the training analysis as an illustra-
tion of the inherent contradiction present in any attempt to impose
strict rules on the analytical relationship. It is, in fact, the norm
rather than the exception for professional relationships to become
personal upon analytic termination, a fact which clearly runs
counter to our ethics of the transference. Building on this paradox,
Zoja asks a series of questions which can only be answered by the
passage of time.

In The Dilemma of the Analyst, the Healer, and the
Community, our focus turns to the challenges and difficulties in the
interactions and responsibilities of the individual professional and
the community. All of the earlier essays highlight the fact that there
is both a dilemma and a tension in the relationship of the practitioner to the community in which she or he functions. The essays
in this section take more specific looks at both the dilemmas and
possible resolutions to them. Focusing more specifically on sexual
acting out by the analyst in "Analysis: Ritual without Witnesses,"
Fred Plaut sees a way out of the dilemma of the tension between
individual and community. He assigns that dilemma in analytical
psychology to the misapplication of the transference, as depicted
through the *Rosarium Philosophorum*, to individual psychology,
suggesting that in our highly individualistic manner, Jungians have
used the symbol of the *coniunctio* as applying solely to the inner
life. Plaut instead argues for understanding it as a cultural phenomenon which needs to be put into context in the framework of an
important ritual of our contemporary civilization and for seeing it
instead as "reciprocity in relatedness," thus including the individual
within the context of his or her culture.

The idea of analysis as ritual is an intriguing one, and it is
picked up in the next essay, "Ethics in Xhosa Healing." We are fortunate to have a paper focusing on a non-Western group of healers
written by M. Vera Bührmann and G. S. D. Davis. Bührmann has

worked for years with the Xhosa of South Africa, where "ritual specialists" are among the healers who tend to the spiritual and psychic health of members of the community. In this group, the function of healers is ritualized as a part of community life, and no healing of the individual is attempted without the involvement of the entire family. Confidentiality obviously cannot be a part of their particular code; instead, containment is maintained by the strict observance of ritual behavior. Here, the ritual aspect of the healer discussed by Plaut is an actual part of the culture. Additionally, the healers view themselves as the servants of the ancestors, thus avoiding hubris, a flaw which Zoja mentions. In this culture, sickness is viewed as a matter which affects the entire group, the healing of which involves the entire group as well.

When discussing ethical judgments, it is almost impossible not to notice that often when a community is called upon to judge a colleague, the worst opportunities arise for aberrant behavior by the judges. Unfortunately, such situations often seem to occasion sanctioned methods for turning on a colleague, sometimes in a brutal way. Verena Kast addresses this issue in her essay, "How to Handle Unethical Behavior in an Ethical Way." While acknowledging, as many essays in this book do, the necessity of regulating collegial behavior in some way, Kast also analyzes the pitfalls for the investigators. Those who are called upon to decide the facts and assign punishment run into the difficulty of losing relatedness as their shadows become activated. The ethic of relation, underscored previously by Haule and Plaut in other ways, is at the center of a search for some understanding of the dangers that may befall the pursuers. It is also presented as a means to bridge the gap between personal and collective ethics.

Joseph Wakefield's "Am I My Brother's Keeper? Impairment in the Healing Profession" continues this theme. Here, the author begins with a painful and personal recognition of both impairment and its denial by the group, which he experienced directly as a result of the alcoholism in his own family while he was growing up. Through this early experience, he was able to recognize what such denial can do to a group and to the impaired person. As a result, Wakefield is strongly in favor of confronting the impaired individual for the sake of both himself or herself and the community. He proposes a model which emphasizes health and rehabilitation rather than impairment or disability and holds with the belief that the impaired individual can be restored to health.

The final section of our book is entitled, Behind Ethics: Archetypal Structures. Archetypes, those psychological components most associated with Jung, lie behind diverse approaches to ethics, and in this concluding part of the book, the authors address the larger backdrop which acts as an organizing factor for ethical thinking. Throughout this section, how Eros energy is handled by analysts, specifically when it is acted out, provides the starting point for the essays. No essay heretofore has addressed the question of what occurs in the actual treatment of the practitioner who has strayed and acted out sexually with a client. Manisha Roy's paper, "Psyche's Punishment: Holding the Tension Between Spirit and Instinct," is a frank and moving portrait of an analysis conducted on just these grounds. Roy allows us to follow her in a journey with her patient through the excruciating punishment that psyche has waiting for "Ann," who has had an affair with a client thirty years her junior. Guided as well as punished throughout by Ishtar, her long, sad journey also held the promise of healing. Roy's poignant tale is set in the theoretical framework of the ongoing struggle between spirit and instinct. Roy sees how the failure of the analyst to remain in the tension of the conflict is then compounded by the failure of the community, who cannot trust enough in psyche to allow its punishment to work. The case is offered as a sample of what can happen when the twin failures do not materialize.

Maria Teresa Rufini's essay, "The Handless Maiden: Ethics as the Transcendent Function," acts as a pure archetypal complement to Roy's paper. Through this fairy tale, Rufini shows a schemata of an incest situation wherein the only hope for true recovery of self lies in the maiden's ability to descend alone into depths, to "recompense the eruption of evil." Rufini's thesis has to do with the maturing effect of endurance and suffering. This psychological condition provides the context within which the transcendent function can manifest, reconciling incompatible opposites. Rufini interprets the tale as an indicator that the emergence of the transcendent function happens only through an intense inner experience, not through assigning of blame, of which there is plenty. Here, the appearance of the transcendent function signals that a *tertium* has emerged, "evil" has been defeated, and life can now continue. For Rufini, as for Roy, the necessary path for healing lies away from affixing culpability and towards "detachment and silence."

In Rosemary Gordon's paper, "Transference-Countertransference: The Eros-Agape Factor," she strives for a balance between these two energies which are connected but represent differing aspects of love. Using clinical material, Gordon indicates how important it is for the analyst to include both facets yet strive not to give too much emphasis to either one, as a balance of the two is necessary for healing. The understanding of how Eros and agape affect the transference and countertransference might, Gordon feels, enable the analyst not to act out or, on the other hand, not to resort to legalistic, cold mechanisms in the analysis. Finally, Gordon reminds us that for the practitioner who infringes the ethical code, Jesus' direction (as implied in the tale of the adulteress) is for each of us to "develop there our [own] trial and verdict." The first three essays in this section all arrive at a similar model: the inward journey, no matter what actions may be taken in the outer world, may be, in the end, what matters.

A further look into how sexual acting out occurs, and how we are to understand its causes, can be found in John Steinhelber's essay, "The Healing *Coniunctio* and Its Sexual Romantic Shadow." Like Plaut, Steinhelber feels that Jung's alchemical model of the transference/countertransference can be misapplied or misinterpreted. While Plaut sees the problem in a lack of a ritual container, Steinhelber views the trouble as having to do with the shadow inherent in Jung's alchemical opus and our failure to work with that shadow, both individually and as a community. Making use of three poignant examples from clinical practice, he is able to move us through the three stages of Jung's *coniunctio*, indicating what was intended in each case and then analyzing what can go wrong and offering possible reasons why. In this way, Steinhelber provides an archetypal basis for understanding both errors in the analyst-patient field as well as support for the healing power of the *coniunctio*.

The archetypal backdrops of this last section exist within one powerful and all encompassing field: that of the Self, the organizing principle behind our conscious and unconscious life. Ann Belford Ulanov, in an essay entitled simply "Self Service," reminds us that everything we do, everything we feel, all of our work must be grounded in devotional submission to this all-embracing reality. Ulanov raises the question of our use of patients to satisfy our own needs in contrast to our service to that which is larger than we are, the Self. Touching on the difficult issues which relate to sexuality, raised throughout this book, Ulanov speaks of them in the context of attempts to reach a kind of loving fulfillment which, if lacking in outer relationships, can only be found through living on "an archetypal level, where we are ushered into the energies of the Self which demand to be realized and lived." In this way, Ulanov believes, "ethical issues ultimately resolve into service to the Self."

III

Ethics are culturally derived boundaries which shift as cultures evolve. They could be said to have emerged as a result of the particular styles of a society, along with the other aspects of life. For example, until recent times, women and people of color were not included as equals in the ethical values of Western culture; women generally have not been included equally in the ethics of most cultures, and children are rarely considered to partake of the natural rights of adults in any culture. There has been a definite, although not uniform, shift in these culturally based ethical systems, however, as societies evolve and become more inclusive. Ethos, the fundamental values of a civilization, represents a prospective element of those evolving ethics, i.e., in what direction the culture as a whole may ultimately be heading. Jung described neurosis in individuals as the sign that a "greater personality" was trying to break through. The tension between personal ethics and community ethics, the balancing of the demands of different cultures and their specific values, can only be resolved through a continuous discourse on the ethics of our times, one which includes many voices, until the emerging ethos, like Jung's "greater personality," can be fully realized.

The Editors
Lena B. Ross and Manisha Roy

Part I

EVOLUTION OF ETHICS

ETHICS AT THE FOUNTAINHEAD

June Singer

My feelings about ethics in analysis were constellated during my four years in Zurich between 1960 and 1964, when I studied and analyzed with men and women who had known Dr. Jung as intimately as people in the Switzerland of that time ever knew one another, people who were trained by Jung and who might be characterized as priests and priestesses of the cult. By this I mean that I hardly ever heard any of these analysts utter a clear negative criticism about Jung, and my impression was that they were deeply committed to teach *his* teachings. Certainly they brought much of themselves to the work, but they tried above all to present Jung to his followers and to provide a "Jungian" experience to their analysands. Among those with whom I had close contact were my own analysts Liliane Frey-Rohn and Heinrich Fierz; my control analysts Fierz, Hans Riklin, Marie-Louise von Franz, director of studies James Hillman, and my thesis advisor, Barbara Hannah. Then there was Dr. Wolfgang Binswanger, who was my supervising analyst when I did my internship at the Sanatorium Bellevue in Kreuzlingen, which was founded by his father, Ludwig Binswanger, the famous existential analyst. All of these, in their various ways— both consciously and unconsciously, deliberately and unwittingly— taught me about the ethics of Jungian analysis. There was much that I questioned about those teachings then, and still more now.

Unfortunately, I never got to discuss any of these matters with Dr. Jung. He died when I had been in Zurich for only a few months. The only time I ever saw him was as he lay on his deathbed upstairs in his home in Kusnacht, dressed in a simple white nightgown, waxen faced in a dim room with candles on either side of him. But his legacy I knew well. It was passed down to me by those who were closest to him.

The wisest statement I ever heard about ethics came from Dr. Fierz, my control analyst. I'd asked him, "How do you know whether what you are doing as an analyst is correct, or ethical?" He responded, "Ask yourself if you would be comfortable about having all of your colleagues know exactly what you were doing. If the answer is yes, no need to worry." I've seen many drafts of a lot of ethics codes since then, but nothing more parsimonious or elegant.

My personal analyst, Liliane Frey-Rohn, was the object of my intensely positive transference. She helped me release my soul from bondage and discovered with me that I had a voice of my own. Naturally, I loved her dearly. She would invite me to dinner once a year at a fine Zurich restaurant, just the two of us. (One wouldn't do that here and now, but I certainly learned a lot from the experience.) I now suppose that she did this with all of her analysands as a sort of ritual, but I never asked whether I was the only one or not. I felt that she regarded me as someone special, not the ordinary analysand, and I didn't want to find out otherwise. Anticipating this annual dinner was the occasion of much excitement and many fantasies. Notwithstanding my heterosexual preference and lifestyle, I imagined bringing her home with me after our dinner and . . . well, I hardly dared to imagine beyond that. I did manage to find the courage to bring up my feelings in analysis, and Liliane made it clear that she found it necessary for her own good and that of the analysand to keep certain boundaries—but she did give me a hug now and then at the end of our sessions. For me, that hug was important, because it symbolized a mutual love which needed to be experienced and expressed, yet contained in the vessel. I don't think it did me any harm.

My late husband, Richard Singer, and I did our training simultaneously in Zurich. I won't say we did it together, because in Zurich analysis was a totally individual matter. You didn't ever do it *with* anybody, in fact, extreme measures were taken to make sure that the one analysis had as little as possible influence on the other. Richard analyzed first with Jolande Jacobi and then with Barbara Hannah, and I know that Liliane Frey-Rohn never spoke to either of them about me or about Richard or asked a single question. He was sealed off from my process, and I was sealed off from his. At a certain point, I asked Liliane if she would see him, because I wanted her to have some objective impression beyond my reports about him, but she adamantly refused. Toward the end of my analysis I completed my thesis with Barbara Hannah as my advisor. We'd talk about the thesis, but never a personal comment or word about my primary relationship ever passed her lips. This pained me very much, because I firmly believed that she had received a warped description of what I was really like, and I had hoped that she might have an opportunity to judge me for herself. It wasn't allowed.

I didn't get any real help on my marital problems because of a certain philosophical stance that pervaded Jungian work then, and perhaps still does, based on the model of the sealed alchemical vessel. It was that the purpose of individuation was to help a person *separate* from the influences of the parents (usually thought of as *flawed*) and to liberate oneself from one's mate, so that one would become independent, self-sufficient and free-standing, and responsible only to the Self. It was surely a parallel to the Newtonian worldview then prevalent in which every thing and every being is seen as a solid substantial entity separate from everything else. Interdependence was not mentioned as a possibility; independence was the goal. All this has changed in the past three decades, during which we have come to accept a worldview based on systems theory and quantum physics where relationship is key and where nothing exists in and of itself but only in relationship.

So Richard and I lived our very separate inner lives together, never knowing what the other was feeling or thinking or dreaming. All these were kept for our respective analysts, whom we trusted, while we regarded each other with curiosity, suspicion, and a feeling of alienation.

There was one exception, but it occurred outside of the Jungian community. Both my husband and I interned at Bellevue. I had been having some particular difficulties with respect to him, so I asked my supervisor, Dr. Binswanger, if I could talk to him about something personal. He said, "What do you want to talk about?" I replied, "It's about my husband." Without so much as a by your leave, Dr. Binswanger picked up the telephone and said, "Send Dr. Richard Singer in here immediately." Anything I had to say had to be said openly in front of my husband. This was my shocking introduction to relationship therapy. The alchemical vessel broke wide open, and for once both of us could see what was inside. I recognized the vessel as a can of worms, but better outside than inside. Ethical? Yes, I think so. But the shibboleth of confidentiality no longer protected either of us, nor could we hide behind our analysts' skirts. We had to face what was real.

I often wondered what Jung's relationships were like. I wondered how intimate he had been with those adoring women with whom he surrounded himself, whom he trained and who became his admiring acolytes. I asked Dr. Frey-Rohn about this but never got a straight answer. Always something vague that almost led me to believe she had a special relationship with Jung, but that none of the others did. But did they all grant such veiled assumptions? As to Toni Wolff, in those days the cat was not yet out of the bag, and the analysts would only indicate that one didn't talk about that relationship. But, of course, all the training candidates did. There was always so much secrecy. I'm not sure that confidentiality and secrecy are the same thing. I have always wondered how many ethical breaches are concealed under the rubric of confidentiality.

While I was in Zurich, there was a big scandal involving one of the male analysts. The husband of one of this analyst's analysands sued him for seducing his wife. Despite all attempts on the part of the institute to hush up the matter, it came to court. The analyst lost the case and had to pay damages to the woman (or maybe it was to the woman's husband, I'm not sure which). The analyst did not have the grace to resign from the institute, nor did the curatorium, the institute's governing body, put pressure on him to leave. The word that got around the institute was that the offending analyst was not fired because he knew about certain indiscretions on the part of other male members of the curatorium. I asked my own analyst about this, and she said she had advised the analyst to leave town for a year or two until the episode could "blow over." I was incensed but said nothing more.

We were never taught anything specifically about ethics in

our seminars at the institute as far as I can recall. Most of what we learned about transference/countertransference was based on Jung's commentary on the *Rosarium Philosophorum*. Of course, we understood that this was all symbolic—you were not supposed to get into the bathtub with your analysand—but after the symbolism came and went, what actually was permissible? Somehow, with the conferring of the analyst's diploma, you were supposed to know.

Many years later, I requested an audience with Barbara Hannah at one of the IAAP Conferences. I told her about myself and my relationship with Richard, who had died shortly after completing analytic training. When she'd had an opportunity to hear me out, she was amazed and admitted openly that if she had known what I was really like, the course of Richard's analysis would have been very different. Also years later, after I had learned that I had been betrayed while in Zurich by another training candidate who also was her analysand, I confronted Liliane Frey-Rohn and asked her, "How is it that you knew that I was being betrayed by this person and you never said anything to me, nor did you encourage this person to behave in a more ethical way toward me?" My analyst implied that while her analysand's behavior was bad for me, it was good for her analysand's individuation. I told Dr. Frey-Rohn I thought this was wrong, and all she could say was, "What would you have done?"

I feel that my training in Zurich was sorely lacking in the area of ethics. As a result, when I started my own analytic practice in Chicago, where, after Richard's death, I was the only Jungian analyst for several years, I floundered around and made my own mistakes. I learned from bitter experience that being an analyst is hard and lonely, that if you are going to do this work the needs and interests of analysands must come before those of the analyst, and that if the analyst cannot cope with this, then she or he had better not work with these individuals. I also learned that we analysts can deeply love some of our analysands, but that it is best that we keep this reality to ourselves.

June Singer, *Ph.D., is a Jungian analyst in private practice in Palo Alto, California. She is a member of the C.G. Jung Institute of*

San Francisco and was a founder of the Jung Institute of Chicago and the Inter-Regional Society of Jungian Analysts. She is the author of the following books: The Unholy Bible: Blake, Jung, and the Collective Unconscious; Boundaries of the Soul: The Practice of Jung's Psychology; Androgyny: The Opposites Within; Energies of Love; Seeing Through the Visible World: Jung, Gnosis, and Chaos; *and* A Gnostic Book of Hours: Keys to Inner Wisdom.

EROS, MUTUALITY, AND THE "NEW ETHIC"

John R. Haule

To look at an issue psychologically is to place psyche and its life at the center of our concern, where neurotic symptoms are the attempt of a "greater personality" to break through. But in the realm of ethics, we often fear that the "greater personality" may foster anarchy. Even Jung distanced himself from Erich Neumann's classic essay, *Depth Psychology and a New Ethic* (1949), despite its sober articulation of the tension between the demands of the collective and those of the Self. Although unsurpassed in its simplicity and persuasiveness, Neumann's formulation is not easily applied to the psychotherapeutic interaction, for it has nothing to say of mutuality: the fact that *two* "greater personalities" are trying to emerge out of the same process. After summarizing Neumann's argument, I shall enlarge it to include mutuality.

Neumann distinguishes three modes of ethical living: the "average" individual under the "old ethic," the "elite" under the "old ethic," and those who follow a "new ethic." Under the old ethic, a moral leader privy to a numinous "voice" (Moses, the prophets, Jesus, Paul, Muhammad, the Buddha, Confucius) articulates and codifies a set of rules for right behavior that establishes a secure and dependable social order. Average individuals simply follow these rules, thereby developing a morally respectable persona and suppressing a reprehensible shadow. They gain a conscience but tend to identify with persona and deny the shadow, resulting in inflation and scapegoating.

The elite of the old ethic are consciously and actively involved with the same codified precepts to which the average are more passively subject. The saints of Judaism, Christianity, and Islam typically identify with the shadow and hold themselves guilty of the greatest sins. In this way they obviate scapegoating and deflate their ego at the same time that they expand its scope. When they avoid masochism and pretense, their introspective style achieves a higher consciousness, a much more sensitive conscience, and a far more individual moral agency than that of the non-elite. They are more psychological but still without "depth," for they know nothing of the unconscious or individuation. Their ethic is founded entirely on consciousness.

The *new* ethic is made possible by the insights of depth psychology, where "wholeness" has replaced "perfection" as the goal of moral striving. Whereas under the old ethic "good" was defined by ego's submission to a collective code, the new ethic declares: "Whatever leads to wholeness is 'good'; whatever leads to splitting is 'evil'" (Neumann 1949, p. 126). The voice—no longer the exclusive property of a great leader—speaks as the Self within each individual and may very well direct us contrary to precepts of the old ethic. Indiscriminate approval of everything voiced, however, does not define new-ethic morality. Rather, the individual is required to suffer an inner conflict between demands of the Self and those of the collective. There ensues a self-questioning in which the ego's dialogue partner is not the graven tablet of a collective code but the wholeness of the psyche in its multiform fluidity.

I have nothing to add to Neumann when it comes to sketching out relations between psychology and ethics. Still, it is one thing to sketch and another to apply what is sketched to the convoluted problems of real life. Let us consider the issue of romantic/sexual feelings that arise between analyst and analysand during the course of their work. Let us further, for the sake of argument, eliminate all question that the analyst is lecherous, inexperienced, or obviously lacking in boundaries. Without eliminating the possibility of neurotic issues in either party, let us assume earnest sincerity and a love of truth on both sides. Finally, let us make it the hardest case of all, the one Jung describes in "The Psychology of the Transference" (1946), the infrequent instance when the analysis becomes overwhelmingly urgent for *both* parties.

We expect it to be central for the analysand; but when the analyst is drawn this profoundly in a romantic direction, a difficult pass has indeed been reached. At the present day, there can be no doubt of a collective ethical code. The average old-ethic analyst can proceed with confidence, repressing the voice, taking consolation from an identification with the collective superego, and feeling immensely superior to heinous colleagues who are sometimes sued for seeming to flaunt the code. The average old-ethic analyst may have to exercise heroic self-restraint but is rewarded with a hero's inflation.

The situation is not so comfortable for the elite old-ethic analyst. This professional feels tremendously defeated by the very fact of falling in love with an analysand. To have a numinous inner voice urging a flagrant violation of collective values seems to prove the analyst guilty, weak, incompetent, and "unanalyzed." The erotic feelings that fill the consulting room may very well drive such an analyst into a second analysis and more intensive supervision in order to get to the bottom of the shadow issues. Elite old-ethic analysts feel compassion for and tend to identify with fallen colleagues whose trials make the front pages of the newspapers. They themselves have been saved only by the grace of God.

For both types of old-ethic analyst, the message of the voice is unimportant—its significance deriving entirely from its formal role as tempter. Furthermore, the analysand's situation requires no discussion. The code's concern to protect the less powerful member of the analytic dyad affords the old-ethic analyst the luxury of believing that what is good for the collective is necessarily also good for this particular analysand.

The new-ethic analyst demolishes old certainties with two radical assumptions: that the voice must always be listened to— though not always followed—and that the analysand might not conform to collective expectations. The Self is a trickster sage, unpredictable, inexhaustible, and dangerous when taken seriously. Its voice is as rarely introduced into discussions of ethics in psychotherapy as "promptings of the Holy Spirit" are into Christian ethics. Indeed, to speak of valuing Self at all, in this context, is to open oneself to the suspicion of being an advocate for sexual acting out between analyst and analysand. I therefore regret having to say what should be obvious, that I do *not* advocate misconduct and that the proscriptions of the code reflect the wisdom of a *consensus gentium* which deserves deep respect—even if some of its champions are hysterical proponents of an average old-ethic mentality.

Because two individuation projects are at stake, the ethical problem cannot be viewed in terms simply of an inner dialogue between the ego and self of the analyst. There is also a dialogic tension between ego and self in the analysand, as well as another between the two individuals. Once we eliminate the collective code as a point of departure for psychological approach to ethics, we are forced to look upon interpersonal issues with new seriousness. Mutuality, the oneness that obtains between two or more individuals engaged in the same process, must be central to our discussion.

Self is the key to understanding mutuality, for it is not only the ground of *my* wholeness but also of *ours*. Self is not a personal possession, separate in each individual, but rather the greater reality in which we all participate. In Jung's metaphor, it is the rhizome, the root structure shared by two flowers that only seem separate because they emerge from different locations on the surface of the soil (Jung 1952, p. xxiv). Self is the matrix out of which the myriad instances of individual consciousness emerge.

The interpersonal Self field in which we all move may seem irrelevant to our morning rush to catch the 7:09. But when we find ourselves in a powerfully archetypal relationship, evidence of mutuality moves to the foreground of our awareness. Romantic love, analytic transference, motherhood, and the like, are characterized by a profound sense of being linked—even united. "Telepathic" and other synchronistic experiences are relatively common. The Self field seems to act as a kind of unconscious channel of communication between analyst and analysand. Furthermore, it participates in these relationships as a kind of third partner. It is the dyad and yet greater than the dyad, having an autonomy of its own. It cannot be deliberately manipulated by either analyst or analysand. It is, in short, a third manifestation of the trickster sage. I, as analyst, am aware of an inner dialogue with my wholeness which is different from your dialogue, to which I am not directly privy—although you, the analysand, may tell me about it. In addition to this, we are aware of being in trialogue with a process which is neither "mine" nor "yours" but "ours."

These considerations reveal the complexity of ego-Self relations as they occur in analysis. The analyst's moral choices, if they have integrity, cannot afford to ignore any of the dialogues comprising the ego-Self relation. To illustrate the intricacy of moral decision-making for a new-ethic analyst whose voice seems to be advocating romantic involvement with an analysand, I shall imaginatively place myself in that predicament. We assume a reciprocity of feelings and that both parties are sincere, as honest with themselves as they can be, and not particularly neurotic.

The voice brings with it a numinous fatefulness and sense of moral obligation that cannot be mistaken for a passing fancy. I have a sense that this relationship is the climax to which my life has been leading, where the strands of my past find fulfillment. There is no doubt in my mind that if this woman were not my analysand, I would throw myself wholeheartedly into adventure with her. But I am not inexperienced at this; I know I could be mistaken about the voice or its intentions. I therefore examine my dreams and incidental daytime fantasies or mood swings and especially review the history of my intimate relationships, taking a close look at whatever patterns emerge.

Like the elite old-ethic analyst, I need to get better acquainted with my shadow and the inflation that goes with being the hearer of a voice. I know that encounter with an archetype is always numinous and "divinely ordered." Experience has shown me several cases of analysts who sincerely believed themselves exceptions to the collective code, and I have had some of their analysand-lover casualties as patients. I investigate whether I might not be as deluded as they were. I deflate my ego by assembling a host of unfavorable comparisons with these fallen shadows and search for evidence whether this may not be the most adequate context in which to place my palpitating heart. The labyrinthine darkness of this introspection is likely to lead me into a second analysis with a new-ethic analyst who is able to tolerate the tension of such collectively forbidden reflections.

Meanwhile, I am obliged empathically to encourage a similar rigor in my analysand's self-examination. Deep and honest dialogue is all the new-ethic analyst has for ascertaining a moral course. But the insistent press of instinctual forces works to short-circuit it. Therefore, keeping all lines of communication open is my first responsibility. Furthermore, as her analyst, I am in good position to draw numerous conclusions about possibly neurotic and symbolic meanings in my analysand's infatuated transference. These, too, have to be added to my own inner dialogue, for it is the analyst's burden to have to pay attention to *two* individuation projects. What is not individuating for her cannot be a morally proper choice for me.

Another important area of investigation I cannot afford to overlook would be the actual course of events in our sessions. Is the process moving naturally, or has our emotional overload brought it to a halt? Are we obstructing autonomous expressions of the unconscious in our desire to draw a wished-for conclusion? Experience has taught me that frequently what starts out as sexual attraction may eventually reveal itself to have a quite different object. Processes that lead us away from a romantic understanding of our attraction must be facilitated. Realistic assessment of my ability to deceive myself may well lead me to find a supervisor who can refrain from directing me without losing the ability to critique my powers of observation and analysis.

The preceding considerations are only preliminary, a method of opening up space for the transcendent function to operate. A depth psychological investigation does not proceed primarily by rational analysis and decision, but by allowing the Self to speak. This means that conflicting options must be clarified and the tension between them borne until what Neumann calls the voice provides a symbol, a flow of energy, or something of the kind. Then this, too, becomes a position from which to have a dialogue.

What has been described so far relates primarily to the individual ego-Self dialogues going on within each of the two participants in the analytic process. Mutuality adds yet another dimension, wherein analyst and analysand operate as the two poles of an interactive field. The identity and inclinations of the two poles must be clear and relatively well-defined before we are in a position to understand and relate to the transcendent function as it manifests in the Self field. Here is the most important arena for the ego-Self dialogue about the nature of the process itself. It is no less complicated, difficult, and liable to self-deception than any of the preliminary dialogues described above.

It is clear, then, that the new-ethic analyst is not relieved of moral responsibility regarding the nature of the analytic relationship and its permutations, but actually loaded with more taxing obligations. It is surely reasonable to think that a morally truthful, mutual decision to end the analysis and begin a romantic liaison would be rare, indeed. But the very fact that the new ethic cannot eliminate the possibility brings cries of outrage from partisans of the old ethic. It is true that the high-minded ethics I have described may be misused by the venal, the juvenile, and the self-deceiving, but no approach to ethics can control the bad faith of certain practitioners. The old ethic hopes to educate them with the wisdom of the *consensus gentium* and coerce them with punishments. The new ethic hopes to remain deeply faithful to psyche.

References

Jung, C. G. 1946. The psychology of the transference. In *Collected Works* 16:163–323. Princeton, N.J.: Princeton University Press, 1966.

_____. 1952. *Symbols of Transformation. Collected Works*, vol. 5. Princeton, N.J.: Princeton University Press, 1967.

Neumann, E. 1949. *Depth Psychology and a New Ethic*. E. Rolfe, trans. New York: G. P. Putnam's Sons, 1969.

John R. Haule *holds a doctorate in religious studies from Temple University and a diploma from the C. G. Jung Institute of Zurich. He is a member of the faculty of the C. G. Jung Institute of Boston and the author of* Divine Madness: Archetypes of Romantic Love *as well as a forthcoming book on emotion and countertransference.*

THE NEED FOR AN ANALYTIC TEMENOS

Florence C. Irvine

In 1991, the Jungian analysts of San Francisco adopted their first ethics code governing the practice of therapists associated with the Society of Jungian Analysts of Northern California, San Francisco. The preamble to the code begins:

> These ethical standards are offered not in the spirit of rules laid down by fiat but of recommendations born out of human experience and human suffering.

A decade earlier, the San Francisco group had rejected the idea of drawing up such a code. It had been feared that the setting out of collective rules would be antithetical to the individual emphasis of Jungian analysis. In 1981, it was felt that codifying expectations for analyst behavior might rigidify practice and drive the shadow underground. Over the next decade, however, the climate changed as a result of extensive experience with the destructive results of sexual boundary violations in analysis. We have learned that a substantial proportion of patients who have been sexually involved with their therapists suffer serious psychological damage (see Pope and Bouhoutsos, 1986, pp. 63–66). While suffering is a necessary part of any analytic work, the kind of psychological injury incurred in a sexual boundary violation is antithetical to healing in that it so frequently results in deepened wounds, stiffened defenses, and a constricted growth potential. Like the survivors of childhood sexual abuse, these patients bring to their subsequent therapists a burden of mistrust, shame, guilt, depression, and a terrible ambivalence concerning the dark secret which they now carry. A recognition of the struggle which such patients face and a wish to prevent such needless suffering were strong motivating forces behind the adoption of the San Francisco Jung Institute's ethics code. In the discussion which follows, I draw upon more than a decade of my own experience as a member of various committees on ethics, well-being, and training in my local psychiatric societies.

Patients need to be free to bring all manner of fantasies and impulses into the analytic situation. We know that the activation of affect and instinct which occurs in a depth analysis has a profoundly stirring effect upon both analyst and analysand. One can readily appreciate the analogy to a chemical (or alchemical) reaction occurring in a glass flask. Chemical reactions, properly contained, result in transformation, often accompanied by great heat and turbulence. Just as the chemist (or alchemist) anticipates the intensity of the reaction and attends to the integrity of the flask, so the analyst must contain and further the transformative processes of the patient through an attention to boundaries, a determination that the process shall serve the needs of the analysand, and a resolve to bring symbolic understanding to what is going on within and between the two psyches in the consulting room. In an intense analytic process, there are frequent opportunities to abandon the analytic stance; as analysts, we must continually remind ourselves and our analysands of the commitment to work symbolically.

Comparable to the analogy of the alchemical flask is the image of the temenos—the sacred space around a temple. Gerhard Adler sees the circle which children draw around themselves and their play objects in therapy as a temenos, a sacred space whose purpose is twofold. The circle prevents dissipation of energy, and it prevents intrusion from the unconscious of the parent (1951, pp. 98–111). The consulting room ideally provides the adult analysand with such a temenos. Because unconscious material is dealt with psychologically, rather than acted out, energy is not dissipated to the outside. Because the analyst takes care to be conscious of the ways in which his or her needs and impulses might intrude upon the process, the psyche of the analysand is allowed to direct the drama which unfolds within the temenos.

Images of a sturdy alchemical flask or of a sacred space exemplify what it is we strive for in the analytic process. Both promote a holding of psychological contents with patience and respect. Both encourage an evolution which proceeds from the analysand, allowing him to retrieve and heal split-off parts of himself. Both pay tribute to the compelling nature of the archetypal world, as well as to the precious individuality of our limited human natures.

How is it, then, that the sacred space of analysis is sometimes violated through an acting out of sexual impulses? I believe that this particular failure results from a tragic coincidence between unconscious factors in analyst and analysand. Since it is the analyst's job to ensure that consciousness is the guiding principle in the work, the responsibility for such a failure rests with the analyst.

In analyses which fail because of sexual acting out, the analysts may offer any of several rationales. They may say that the patient's wound needed an erotic connection in order to be healed, or that there was a need to equalize the power between the analyst and the patient. They may claim that there was a wish to recognize a special quality of intimacy, or that this relationship needed to live in the "real world." Such statements may be sincere, but they are startlingly naive in that they obscure the more shadowy motivations behind the acting out. I believe that the analysts in such cases have become identified with the healer archetype, and this archetypal identification, because it is one-sided and unconscious, blinds them to the need to respect their own and their patient's human limits. It blinds them, as well, to darker and more personal reasons for having allowed the acting out.

Unowned motivations on the part of the analyst may involve a blurring of generational boundaries (the patient fills in as an adoring parent or child), may express a wish to appropriate for oneself the patient's psychic energy, or (in cases of heterosexual involvement) may indicate a hidden hatred of the opposite sex. The analyst may be warding off the analysand's anger or may be expressing impatience with the analysand's depression. Sexual acting out may represent a cynical disrespect for the exacting demands of the analytic vocation. Or the analyst may simply be surrendering to sexual lust.

Any of these darker motivations may hide behind the analyst's avowed belief that the sexual involvement was undertaken in the analysand's best interest. The analyst's position of greater power, combined with intimate knowledge of the analysand's most secret fantasies and hopes, gives access to the patient's inner world as the arena for the enactment of the analyst's own unconscious fantasies. There ensues a terrible confusion of archetypal and personal elements. The temenos is lost, the sacred space is violated.

What are the dynamics of the analysand who has become entangled in this kind of acting out? Analysands are vulnerable to this sort of violation simply because they are invited to regress, to suspend conventional judgments, and to trust, instead, the analyst's judgment in a situation in which powerful archetypal forces are constellated. Most vulnerable of all are those who have actually been abused in earlier life or those in whom there is no reliably internalized protective parental imago.

When a relationship of trust has developed, analysands bring the raw and unfinished parts of themselves to be understood and worked with. When there has been a literal or symbolic incest wound, this, too, will be brought to the analytic container, where it may surface as an apparent demand for literal reenactment (Herman 1992, p. 140). Beneath the surface, there is, if one listens for it, a quieter voice, which pleads for the impulse to be psychologically held, reflected upon, and understood. An apparent bid for sexual connection with the analyst may cover a variety of deeper yearnings on the part of the analysand. There may be a wish to be affirmed as a sexual being. The analysand may be attempting to create the inner experience of childhood, where one can be safely held in the arms of the parent. The analysand may be wrestling with fears of being destructive and may seek to disguise or convert anger into a sexual affair, in order to preserve the connection to the analyst. There may be an attempt to obliterate the space between the two people—a space in which the analysand imagines the analyst's dark judgment lurks.

The nuances of all these impulses and images, coming as they do from deep and forbidden areas of the unconscious, may be terribly difficult to capture in words. As the analysand struggles to understand and express these feelings verbally, an attitude of patient holding is required of both analyst and analysand. By demonstrating a willingness to listen to all voices without being compelled to action, the analyst models for the patient an attitude of conscious restraint. If, instead, the analyst allows the process to be short-circuited by acting out apparently sexual impulses, then the shape of what is seeking to emerge becomes obliterated. The analysand is robbed of the discovery of meaning in his or her own depth experience. The former analytic relationship becomes an affair, a condition more easily attained than some of the other internal relationships with which the analysand has been struggling. Both the personal and archetypal dimensions of the analysand's individual situation become subsumed by this more readily recognizable relationship—the path of least resistance.

Analysands who have become entangled in a sexual relationship with the analyst describe a sense of disappointment, coupled with a guilty need to hide this reaction. Often, there is a shared sense that the analysand should feel grateful for this sign of special favor. In the absence of this response, the analysand is seen as shadowy and wounded, beyond the reach of the analyst's best efforts. If the analyst cannot own the shadow aspects of his or her behavior, and if the patient must continue to idealize the analyst in order to preserve the relationship, then it is the patient who becomes identified with all the darker impulses which precipitated the acting out. The analysand, who may have a history of keeping family secrets, now has yet another to keep. The analysis has failed, and the analysand must add a serious iatrogenic complication to whatever wounds were originally brought for treatment.

A stiffening of psychological structures occurs in response to this betrayal of trust in the analytic process. Often, analysands resort to defenses of dissociation, denial, and psychological constriction in order to deal with the pain of what has befallen them. Perhaps there is the courage to seek another analysis, or perhaps the analysand lives on in a diminished way in silence and isolation. I believe that no one who has witnessed the suffering of even one such analytic casualty can accept the rationales which attempt to excuse sexual acting out in analysis. The damage to the inner life of the analysand—the inner life which we claim to respect and nurture—is simply too great.

We need to recognize that none of us is immune from the

temptation to cross sexual boundaries in the course of analytic work. We must be alert to the warning signs which precede such boundary violations (see Pope and Bouhoutsos 1986, pp. 166–167), and we must know to seek immediate consultation with a knowledgeable colleague or with an ethics committee. As colleagues, we must be prepared to offer understanding and compassion to those who seek us out as consultants. We must also be able to say unequivocally: "Sexual contact by a therapist with a patient is a breach of ethics—*always.*"

The temenos develops from a decision made by the analyst at the outset of the work. The Latin roots for the word *decide* are the verb "to cut" and the preposition "away from." When we decide to take someone into an analytic relationship, we consciously cut ourselves away from other forms of relationship with that person. We do this out of respect for the analysand's potential wholeness. In this regard, I find it helpful to remember Jung's statement: "The feeling for the infinite . . . can be attained only if we are bounded to the utmost" (1961, p. 325). By limiting ourselves to an analytic relationship, we paradoxically allow the analysand the most unlimited freedom to explore the depth and breadth of the psyche.

References

Adler, G. 1951. Notes regarding the dynamics of the self. *Spring*, pp. 98–111.

Herman, J. L. 1992. *Trauma and Recovery.* New York: Basic Books.

Jung, C. G. 1961. *Memories, Dreams, Reflections.* New York: Vintage Books.

Pope, K. S., and J. C. Bouhoutsos. 1986. *Sexual Intimacy Between Therapists and Patients.* New York: Praeger.

Florence C. Irvine, *M.D., is an Assistant Clinical Professor at the University of California in San Francisco and a member of the teaching faculty of the C. G. Jung Institute of San Francisco. She has served on the Well-being Committee of Northern California Psychiatric Society and on the Ethics Committee of the C. G. Jung Institute of San Francisco.*

Part II

METATHEORIES OF ETHICS

THE SCHEHERAZADE SOLUTION

POWER ABUSE AND AN ETHIC OF
TRANSFORMATION

Lena B. Ross

What do we talk about when we talk about ethics in psychotherapy? Usually we are considering sexual relations between analyst and analysand or between analyst and candidate. We may be curious about sex between colleagues, but rarely as a matter of ethics. It is the perceivable imbalance in power that catches our attention and turns a sexual liaison into a matter for ethical judgment. General consensus has certainly been reached on the matter of acting out sexually, which is universally realized to be harmful and certainly not a desirable outcome of "therapy." However, sexual acting out is an easily identifiable subset of a larger issue: *imbalance in power relations between individuals and within groups.* Here the issues are often ill defined, as they do not fit into the structure of our clear-cut rules and strict punishments. In the absence of sexual acting out, rules do not apply quite so easily to power abuses between analysts and analysands, candidates and analysts, students and teachers, supervisors and supervisees, etc., and yet these abuses often have long-ranging destructive consequences.

The origins of our particular ethical system, which derive

from the consolidation of masculine consciousness in post-Neolithic times, may be part of the cause of these power abuses. Patriarchally organized cultures produced rigid responses to violations, exemplified in such systems as the Code of Hammurabi, Mosaic law, Confucianism, or Shari'a, the code of Islamic law. Over the years, rules and regulations, punishments and ostracisms, have proliferated in an attempt to control perceived violations of ethics, but despite the development of more and more codes, breaches seem to occur with depressing regularity.

Of course, this does not mean that we don't need guidelines for social behavior, but it indicates that the specific rules resulting from an emerging patriarchal culture don't always work. Since the culture defines the rules, abuses which do not have a concrete manifestation are often not clearly seen *as* violations. In order for power abuses to become visible, outside of the concrete realm of sexual acting out or financial misappropriation, the lens through which we view our behavior needs to change.

I wonder whether there may be an inherent fallacy in trying to derive the solution from the culture which evinced the problem originally. In fact, these very rules might act to obscure sadism in power relations, much less help to define and heal. Is it possible that systems such as those previously mentioned, by their very rigidity, actually *encourage* bullying in areas such as training or the judging of others in our community, for example? Enantiodromia, "the emergence of the unconscious opposite in the course of time" (Jung 1921, par. 709), would almost guarantee such an outcome. The rigidity of rules developed to control ethical abuse *as defined in a particular system* could, in turn, provide cover for abuse of another sort.

I have been working with ancient texts, primarily fiction, for a long time, so I asked myself whether they might contain ways of "seeing" which differ from the ways of the current culture. Jung's theories of compensatory phenomena have provided a clue to understanding the significance of certain literary material, appearing at the dawn of written fiction, which did not seem to be an expression of the prevailing cultural dominant. Jung describes compensation as "an inherent self-regulation of the psychic apparatus . . . I regard the activity of the *unconscious* (q.v.) as a balancing of the one-sidedness of the general *attitude* (q.v.) produced by the function of *consciousness*" (1921, par. 694). He goes on to say that "the activity of consciousness is *selective*. Selection demands *direction*. But direction demands the *exclusion of everything irrelevant*" (ibid.). Applying this thinking to the development of culture, surely any psychic data which ran counter to the imperative of the new dominant could be termed "irrelevant" and relegated to the unconscious level.

Through literature, psyche offered material which could indicate alternative attitudes and methods for handling transgressions. As written manuscripts containing *formal* literature (e.g., scripture, heroic poetic cycles, odes) emerged all over the world expressing the values of the dominant culture, compensatory consciousness began to emerge also in such early written tales as the widow of Ephesus episode from Petronius Arbiter's *Satyricon* (1 A.D.). Here, a widow is at a tomb mourning the death of a beloved husband. A soldier is also present whose task is to guard the bodies of three crucified wrongdoers in order to make sure they are not stolen. If one should be stolen on the soldier's watch, the rigid rules of the state prescribe that he must be crucified in place of the missing body. The widow and guard fall in love, and while they are making love, a body is stolen. The soldier despairs, but the widow "saves her lover by proposing the crucifixion of her husband's corpse. For Petronius's narrator this action adds outrageous impiety to sexual immorality," but the woman's behavior is life-seeking, a "creative initiative in the given situation" (Grossman 1980, pp. 115–116). The widow chooses life over death.

Other examples of compensatory heroic consciousness are demonstrated through figures such as Psyche in Apuleius's *Golden Ass* (second century C.E.), who learns to disobey both the human collective and the gods in order to pursue her path. Or Kaguya-hime, from the earliest known fictional manuscript in Japan, *Taketori Monogatari* (ninth century C.E.), disobedient in her firm rejection of any union with men, even her emperor. There is Dhat al-Himma, from the eponymous folkloric epic cycle, an Arabic warrior woman representing change from the Umayyad through ᶜAbbasid periods (seventh to ninth century C.E.), who fought to unite her desert people in her own way under the banner of Islam. These tales are not the only ones to offer striking differences in direction from patrifocal culture.

Out of the tales I have studied, I have chosen *Alf Layla Wa Layla*, which first appeared in manuscript form in the ninth century. In the West it is referred to as *The Arabian Nights*, and I have choosen it because it exemplifies an alternative paradigm in a situation where abuse of power and its catastrophic consequences are apparent. An archetypal pattern is offered through these tales which differs radically from such structures as the Yahwehistic fear and judgment based point of view or the rules of Christianity and Islam which developed from them. *The Arabian Nights* suggests instead a more subtle, transformative approach to life which can be applied to ethical dilemmas.

In the story of *The Arabian Nights*, a king and his brother are stunned to find that their wives have been unfaithful. Each brother draws his sword and immediately executes both wives and lovers, but this is not satisfying enough for the powerful King Shâhriyâhr. Each night, he seizes the virgin daughter of a merchant or commoner, sleeps with her, then beheads her in the morning:

> He continued to do this until all the girls perished, their mothers mourned, and there arose a clamor among the fathers and mothers, who called the plague upon his head. (Haddawy 1990, p. 11)

In effect, the king has declared a vendetta against both women and his own people. But by the rules of the culture, the king is all powerful, so apparently no one in the kingdom, not even his vizier, can do anything. It is no coincidence that the king chooses the women from among the least powerful members of his society, the common people. By his acts, Shâhriyâhr has deprived himself and his land of the elements needed for the continuation of life: time, in that neither he nor the women have enough time for dialogue which leads to relatedness; the word, since the fear of death and lack of time leaves the women without words; and new life, which would be the result of procreation and requires time for gestation. Shâhriyâhr, as one critic notes, "by the very act of rendering a female procreative and life-producing, is condemning her to death . . . Eros and Thanatos are fused" (Ghazoul 1980, p. 48).

Into the picture steps Scheherazade, older daughter of the king's vizier, his highest counselor:

She had read the books of literature, philosophy and medicine. She knew poetry by heart, had studied historical reports, and was acquainted with the sayings of men and the maxims of sages and kings. She was intelligent, knowledgeable, wise and refined. (Haddawy 1990, p 11)

As a daughter of nobility, she is exempt from the king's madness. Nevertheless,

> One day she said to her father, "I will tell you what is in my mind . . . I would like you to marry me to King Sharayahr, so that I may succeed in saving the people or perish and die like the rest." Her father refuses to allow this, as he believes she will die, and he attempts to dissuade her with parables, but she says, "Such tales don't deter me from my request . . . . In the end, if you don't take me to [the king], I shall go to him myself behind your back and tell him that you refused to give me to one like him and that you have begrudged your master one like me." (Ibid., p. 15)

Her father, afraid of the king's anger, gives in to her blackmail.

Scheherazade has a plan that I would describe as follows: since the rules of the kingdom imbue the king with omnipotence, she must transform him into a partner rather than an all-powerful dominator. How she does this is the basis of the entire text. Her intent to reeducate the king, as well as her method, is clear from the beginning, as she goes to her younger sister, Dînârzâd, and says,

> "Sister, listen well to what I am telling you. When I go to the king, I will send for you, and when you come and see that the king has finished with me, say, 'Sister, if you are not sleepy, tell us a story.' Then I will begin to tell a story, and it will cause the king to stop his practice, save myself and deliver the people." (Ibid.)

When she is with the king, Scheherazade spins a long narrative of tales within tales, each one of which she deliberately stops just at dawn, so that the king, who is enthralled, lets her live another day to finish the tale. Her narrative embodies the principle of *aja'ib*, or astonishment. This technique, which requires *sabr*, or patience, is specifically designed to introduce a symbolic attitude. It is the new attitude which will stop the destruction, remold the king's point of view, and transform through creative narration. Through her tales, Scheherazade creates a new discourse, heretofore impossible. She stops time through her narration, in effect deliberately inserting a prolonged pause between the impulse and the action and thus transforming the king's vengeful, literal, all-or-nothing impulses. It is this which allows the development of a symbolic mode.

In patristic mythologies, the god or gods who create humans often wipe out their products when the direction of the race is unsatisfactory, as if the people cannot be redeemed (as in the flood mythology found in both the Bible and the Koran). But in the model offered by Scheherazade, time is neutralized instead, so the destructive energy which Shâhriyâhr represents can be trans-formed and eventually redeemed. Scheherazade represents a *process* version of new creation, a *trans*formative rather than for-mative dimension. With the "Scheherazade solution," a transforma-tion of the old becomes possible through Scheherazade's ability to generate a continuous stream of tales. This represents her capacity to provide new life in a different way, by a path which avoids the continuous loop of destruction and replacement.

Compare the Scheherazade solution to the central, patriar-chal myth of the old king vs. the new king, where the death of the old king is desirable in order for the new king to assume his place and continue the life of the kingdom. Psychologically, we would ordinarily regard this as symbolic of a new ruling principle replac-ing the old, worn-out ruling principle in the psyche. However, the rising and killing and replacement is cyclic; it forms a feedback loop with an unfortunate tendency to foster the very problems it seeks to prevent. Culture can become stuck in a single pattern, temporarily losing its elasticity, the necessary capacity to evolve. The Scheherazade solution, with its emphasis on time and dis-course, provides an alternative route which maintains the primacy of the symbolic dimension.

The Arabian Nights also contains considerable evidence that supports its own greater symbolic import. The Arabic title actu-ally translates as "One Thousand Nights and One Night." Subsequent translators took this literally and added hundreds of tales that were not originally in the text (the earliest extant manuscript covers only 271 nights, despite the title), but the number one thousand and one was commonly used in the Middle East to refer to infinity. The meaning of this symbol of the infinite may be that transformation requires infinite patience and that whatever time is required can be made available. Additionally, Ferial Jabouri Ghazoul points out that the number 1,001 in binary mathematics (commonly used in the ancient Middle East) equals nine in our decimal system. As Ghazoul notes, nine is the number of months of pregnancy. Although she calls this an esoteric reading of the title, it appears to be further proof that the text presents a compensatory mode of new life, one in which a psychological rebirth is anticipated.

The text itself is rife with etymological indications of change. In the first half of the manuscript, for example, the words which are used to express desire refer only to the physical, sexual aspect or to urges like urination and defecation over which one has little control—such as *waqa'a*, from the trilateral root *w-q*, meaning to mount; *jama'a* from the trilateral root *j-m-c*, meaning to lay; and *qada*, from the root *g-d-q*, meaning to satisfy—all of which place desire on the bestial level. In contrast, words used in the later tales reflect the expression of desire in the sense of union, such as *hawa*, from the trilateral root *h-w-y*, a word which means love in the sense of attachment, an inclination of the soul or mind towards another.

There is ample evidence in the text to underline the message of the story of Scheherazade. The internal tales adumbrate in a multitude of ways the thrust of her message, that saving the "kingdom" means far more than killing and replacing the king. Her approach underscores the possibility of retaining the energy represented by the king, *but transformed*; destroying him is never an option. A Scheherazade attitude might be effective in those situations we view or should view as ethical dilemmas.

For instance, how might psychotherapists using a Scheherazade attitude view the dynamic with which we train people: the fear, unspoken and unaddressed (or the fear that is spoken of but seen as the candidates' complexes), with which psychoanalytic candidates are controlled? Could we organize our professional societies in partnership rather than in a hierarchal way, and could this produce a change in our power relations? When colleagues are charged with violating community standards, would a Scheherazade attitude give us another vantage point from which to understand what our responses need to be? It is a Scheherazade attitude that actually transforms in analysis, and I wonder whether we can afford to do less in terms of our own behavior towards transgressors.

To consider adopting such a paradigm is to think through a broad and general change in the way we psychotherapists approach ourselves, our colleagues, our patients, and particularly our candidates, in terms of power relations and the abuses that are generated because of them. I believe we may be working from an antiquated system of ethics which focuses on the most concrete and easily definable aspects of human power, while ignoring the larger question of what power relationships are and what they do to people. The slower and more difficult route embodied through the metaphor of Scheherazade requires creativity, patience, and a profound belief in the inevitable movement of the unconscious. I believe it presents another archetypal possibility which could be applied in a different conception of ethics.

References

Adlington, W., trans. 1566. *The Golden Ass; Being the Metamorphoses of Lucius Apuleius.* Revised by S. Gaselee. Cambridge, Mass.: Harvard University Press, Loeb Classical Library Edition, 1915.

cAli b. Musa al-Maqanibi et al., eds. 1980. *Sirat al-Amira Dhat al-Himma.* Beirut: al-Maktaba al-Thaqatiyya.

Ghazoul, Ferial Jabouri. 1980. *The Arabian Nights: A Structural Analysis.* Cairo: National Commission for UNESCO.

Grossman, Judith. 1980. Infidelity and fiction: The discovery of women's subjectivity in Arabian Nights. *Georgia Review* 34(1).

Haddawy, Husain, trans. 1990. *The Arabian Nights.* Based on the text edited by Muhsin Mahdi. New York: W. W. Norton and Co.

Jung, C. G. 1921. Definitions. *CW* 6:408-486. Princeton, N.J.: Princeton University Press, 1989.

Lane, E. W. 1984. *Arabic/English Lexicon*. Cambridge, England: Islamic Text Society.

Petronius. *Satyricon*. W. H. D. Rouse, trans. Harvard: Harvard University Press, Loeb Classical Library, 1913.

Rimer, T. 1988. *Modern Japanese Fiction and Its Traditions*. Princeton, N.J.: Princeton University Press.

Lena B. Ross, *Ph.D., is a Jungian analyst in private practice in Manhattan and the Director of Studies for the Center for Analytical Perspectives in New York City, where she is also on the faculty. She is a consultant for the Ms. Foundation for Women, directing the Survivors Fund project, which subsidizes private therapy for adult survivors of incest and childhood sexual abuse. Her first book was* To Speak or Be Silent: The Paradox of Disobedience in the Lives of Women.

ETHICS: A JEWISH PERSPECTIVE

Henry Hanoch Abramovitch

Prophetic vs. Legalistic Mode

The specific difficulty in formulating an ethical perspective for analytical psychology lies in the paradoxical nature of the individuation process itself. Individuation, the process of becoming more and more oneself, implies a necessary distancing from the usual demands of society. Listening to one's inner voice often means blocking out the voices of others, at least for a while, until a balance between inner and outer, surface and depth can be attained. The emphasis on Self, inner voice, individuation, etc., puts the analytical psychologist in what may be called the "prophetic mode." If my inner voice, which I take to be a representative of Self, urges me to do something, I am likely to do it, irrespective of what others may say or feel about such an action. Indeed, the resistance of these "others" may lead me to feel all the more justified in my position.

Ethics, however, are not the exclusive property of the individual but are always shared by the person's community. Societies preserve norms of moral behavior exactly by working out some tacit or explicit agreement on what others believe to be acceptable behavior. Consensus on community standards needs to be hammered out in a "legalistic mode" of rational discourse and collective decision-making, such as majority rule. Under many circumstances, there may be a direct conflict between the individuated "prophetic mode" and the collective "legalistic mode."

Individual vs. Community

One of the basic maxims of Jewish life, which I want by analogy to apply to analytical psychology, is the Hebrew phrase: "kol israel eravim ze le ze" which may be translated as, *"All Jungian analysts are responsible for each other."* Like Jews, Jungian analysts comprise a community. Part of being a community implies the principle of collective responsibility. Just as an action of one Jew, for better or worse, reflects on all Jews, so too an action by one Jungian reflects on the entire Jungian community. That is the price of living in community rather than as a collection of individuals. Just as we may take pride in some achievement by one of our members, so too we must share the burden of the misdeeds, whether we want to or not. In the Jewish perspective, there is no monastic alternative. One must live and die within the "four paces" of community and share in the burden of intra-communal activity. Often, one must submit to the majority of the community, not because they are always right but to preserve the integrity of community. The worse fate for a Jew is not to be part of a community, or to use the biblical metaphor, to be "cut off."

The Fate of Rabbi Eliezer

Many rabbinic stories illustrate the conflict between an individual and his community. One of the most famous involves Rabbi Eliezer b. Hyrcanus, who had a bitter dispute with his colleagues concerning the nature of purity, in this case whether a certain type of clay oven was usable or not. Rabbi Eliezer declared it pure and therefore usable, while the rest of the rabbis declared it impure and to be destroyed. While they were arguing the matter, Rabbi Eliezer appealed, "If I am right, may this tree fly in the air!" and the tree hovered in the air above the ground. But the rabbis said, "In these matters, we do not listen to flying trees." Eliezer went on and cried, "If I am correct, may this stream flow backwards!" and the stream immediately began to flow uphill. But the rabbis said again, "In these matters, we do not listen to streams flowing backwards." Finally, Rabbi Eliezer desperately cried out, "If the *halakha* is with me, may a heavenly voice appear," and a heavenly voice called out, "The *halakha* is with Rabbi Eliezer!"[1] But the rabbis paid no attention, saying once more, "We do not listen to heavenly voices in matters of *halakha*." Rabbi Eliezer did not relent and in the end he was excommunicated. The tragic end to this long drawn out spiritual and ideological conflict was not only his isolation, but his great rage so that "on that day whatever R. Eliezer set his eyes on burst into flames."

The story about Rabbi Eliezer describes just such a transition between a prophetic mode, in which an individual may decide for himself what is right and just, and a legalistic mode, in which individuals must defer to the community standards or be cast out of the community. Jung was, of course, the prophet of analytical psychology and yet certain that his reported actions would violate current community standards. Today, the Jungian community is in the process of a painful transition to a more legalistic mode, in which there is the need to specify clearly and rationally what is permitted and what is forbidden. Undoubtedly, at some future date, we will need the prophets once again.

Sacrificing Individual Happiness

A painful example of how rabbinic law preserves community standards at the expense of individual happiness concerns the breakdown of marriage as a result of an extramarital affair. The common resolution of such an affair in common law today would be to dissolve the first marriage and create the possibility of union between the divorcee and the other man or woman. Rabbinic law sees the matter very differently. It sacrifices the possibility of personal happiness to preserve and sanctify the communal institutions, in this case, the sanctity of marriage. Under circumstances of adultery, a divorce would be mandatory with the proviso that the adulterous pair never see each other again and under no circumstances be allowed to marry. The rabbis saw the danger to the integrity of the family unit if they, as secular courts, were to condone such a practice. Likewise, current analytical norms prohibit sexual relations between analyst and patient. Individual desires are sacrificed to preserve the sanctity of the institution of analysis.

Jewish traditions were very sensitive to the tensions between individual and community, between the prophetic and legalistic modes. Two other stories from Jewish tradition come to mind which reflect the problematic tension between an individual and his community. One story can be found in the Mishnah, a second-century compilation of Jewish law (Eduyot 5:7). Another rabbi, Akavia, son of Mehalalel, resisted the majority opinion on some four points of law. The majority begged him to relent and offered him the presidency of the rabbinical court as an incentive, but he refused. When he was old and about to die, he called his son to him and instructed him as follows: "You must follow the majority on these four points of law. I could not go along with the majority on this issue, since I learned this particular *halakha* from two of my teachers. The other rabbis had learned their version from their two teachers, so each was right to remain adamant in his position. But you, my son, have heard this opinion only from me, a single source, and therefore I insist that in this matter you are required to accept the majority opinion."

This story illustrates what in Jewish tradition has become known as an "ethical will." Such wills do not dispose of material goods but are an attempt to pass on spiritual goods. Often, they are guides to good living in general, but, as in this case, they may be a form of directed address to a specific child. Rabbi Akavia seems acutely aware of his son's dilemma of how to be loyal to his father and yet not suffer his father's fate of being cut off from the community. This father works out a brilliant solution. By his father's command, the son must abide by community standards. In this way, the son is indeed a loyal son but does not carry the dispute into the next generation. Many disputes in practice and theory, in ethics and actions, have their roots in past quarrels. These feuds are then passed on to the next generation so that the "sins of the fathers" become the bitter fruit of the sons, who must choose between the community and their spiritual mentor (or control analyst). Generative leaders, like Rabbi Akavia, leave ethical wills for their children and moral descendants as a guide for good living. I want to suggest that, in the tradition of Rabbi Akavia, generative leaders in analytical psychology consider such ethical wills.

Parable of the King's Son

Another well-known tale is the parable of the king's son by the great Jewish mystic, the Hasid, Rebbe Nachmun of Bratzlav. There was a king who had a son who believed that he was a turkey. He would sit underneath the table, naked, acting like a turkey, eating tidbits which fell underneath the table. None of the doctors were able to cure the king's son. Finally, a man came and said he would be able to do so. He told the king to pay no attention to what he was doing but, at his signal, to pass pants and then shirts underneath the table. The man then took off all his clothes and started acting like the king's son, pretending to be a bird underneath the table. For a while nothing happened. Finally, the king's son noticed the other man and asked him what he was doing underneath the table. The man responded, "I am a turkey." The king's son said, "Oh, I am a turkey as well," and they both resumed their pecking. After a while, the man said, "You know, you can be a turkey, but also wear pants," to which the king's son replied, "Is that so?" The man said, "Yes, indeed," and made the signal for the pants to be passed down. After they had both put on pants, the man went on. "You know, you can be a turkey and even wear a shirt," and he made the signal for the shirt. Later, the man said that one could be a turkey and even eat with a fork. In this way, the man returned the king's son to the community of his father.

Like any good parable, this story is multivocal and constructively ambiguous. For my purposes, I want to focus not on the king's son but on the man who healed him. On the one hand, we know that sometimes we must enter deeply into another person's world in order to bring him back from isolation and madness. We must sometimes cast off persona and join the patient symbolically naked in the bath or under the table. Only in this way are we able to understand his or her world and obtain trust. Although for the healer, this casting off of persona may be part of the healing process, for the society around the healer, such actions can be seen as immoral acts of madness. One can only guess how the king might have said, when the healer took off his clothes, "Who is the crazy one?"

Clearly, there are situations in which unusual, even outrageous, acts are required in the prophetic mode. Jewish tradition recognized situations wherein one is required to violate normal practice, as in cases like *Sophie's Choice*, when to act is to become complicit in an immoral act but not to act is also wrong. In such situations, one should act in such a way as to show that one is acting in unusual circumstances of duress or in some way convey the metamessage that this extraordinary act is *not* a norm of behavior. One device, called "on the other side of the hand," is to perform actions in an unusual manner: if one normally pours coffee right-handed, then under duress does it left-handed, literally, on the other side of the hand. Thereby one gives the metamessage that this action is not normal and not a precedent to follow.[2]

"Justice, justice, you shall pursue!"

This phrase emphasizes the importance of justice. Like Freud's concern with slips, however, the Jewish tradition pays great attention to minor details as having potentially great significance. Hence, the tradition asks, "Why is the word *justice* repeated twice?" One response concerns the nature of justice. It is not enough for justice to be done; it must be done in a way that justice must also appear to be done justly. Justice, therefore, has its inner and outer faces. For justice to work as a guardian of values of doing "what is right and just," the persona of justice must be clean of impurity. If some minor procedure in the administration of justice, such as inadmissible evidence, is violated, then the whole enactment of justice is called into question. Such is, for example, the doctrine of "fruit of the poisoned tree." It is not enough to say "But the person is guilty," he or she must be proved to be guilty in a just way. In this way, details of judicial procedure defend and preserve the entire legal structure and so, ultimately, justice itself.

Jungians like to talk about "the spirit of the work," and I suspect a similar ethos infuses our concerns about dealing with ethical issues and accusations of wrongdoings. The spirit, not the jot and tittle, is important; but the Jewish perspective leads me to emphasize the need for the jot and tittle to embody spirit. "God is in the details" is an oft-heard Jewish phrase, and it makes me think that rather than rely on spirit in matters of ethical violations, we need not only a code of conduct, but a specified series of steps as to how violations of the code are to be addressed, including stages of inquiry, rights of appeal, types of evidence, statute of limitations, etc.

One such procedure in Jewish law includes the need to warn the wrongdoer in advance. This previous warning must, however, be given in a way that the wrongdoer will give heed to the warning. To warn in an ineffective way is a serious offense and may make the person who warns as liable as the wrongdoer. The art of warning seems one that we would do well to cultivate. Warning seems most difficult when the warning must be delivered to a person in a position of power. Here the challenge is to make the powerful person aware of his misdeeds in a way that allows for penance and restitution instead of defensiveness, rationalization, and revenge. In this context, I often think of the story of King David and the prophet Nathan (2 Samuel 12). David seduced another man's wife and, in the cover-up, had her husband killed and then took her for his own. Nathan did not directly criticize David. Instead, he told him a parable about how a rich man with many flocks stole the only lamb of a poor man to provide for a guest. David's anger flared up against the rich man, saying that "the man who did this deserves to die! He must make fourfold restitution for the lamb, for doing such a thing and showing no compassion." Then Nathan said to David, "You are the man . . ." (2 Sam. 12:5–6). This approach allowed for David to confess his sin and accept divine punishment. How to warn well and effectively is as much our moral concern as how to punish the perpetrator. Likewise, again following Jewish traditions, we must have the wisdom to know which misdeeds must be dealt with by a human justice and which left to a Higher Court.

Notes

1. Hebrew, *halakha*, means literally "the way" and is a cognate to the Hebrew verb, "to walk." In practice, the *halakha* is a series of laws and rules which describe in minute detail the actions believers are required to perform.

2. See, for example, Brian Thorne (1987). Thorne, a devout Christian, describes a case in which he was naked with a female patient.

Reference

Thorne, Brian. 1987. Beyond the core conditions. In *Key Cases in Psychotherapy*, W. Dryden, ed. London: Croom Helm.

Henry Hanoch Abramovitch *is a Jungian analyst practicing in Jerusalem. He teaches at the Tel Aviv Medical School, is chairman of the Israeli Anthropological Association, and has advanced degrees from Yale University. He is the author of numerous articles and more recently a book,* The First Father.

REFLECTIONS CONCERNING ETHICS

Luigi Zoja

The ethics of analysis is not a self-contained territory of its own. It is only a special precinct of a larger body of considerations, which is to say that it remains within the sway of the general system of ethics that regulates the whole of our behavior. The absolute principles of that general system constitute the framework to which the ethical code of analysis must always look for orientation.

So it would strike me as futile to discuss specific norms of conduct, or the code that analysts have to respect while exercising their profession, without first having taken a very good look at the general ethical principles from which such a code necessarily descends. We should try to reach a clear understanding of what they are and to ascertain if indeed we hold them in common. These preliminary conditions don't seem to me to have been satisfied. The debate on the ethics of analysis often appears to presume that a shared and unified culture can simply be taken for granted—as though history were somehow motionless and monolithic, or as though all of geography lay focused in a single point. But we know that things stand differently. To give but the simplest of examples, people who are rooted in Catholic and Protestant backgrounds will tend to have different, or even at times opposing, ethical attitudes.

But people who work in the field of depth psychology have to be aware of the general principles on which their ethics rest for reasons that amount to something more than the recognition that a specialized activity has to afford to a more general field of knowledge. It is more than a question of the way in which a civil engineer must never forget the general principles of physics. The analyst's duty is more complex. Depth psychology is a subject as well as an object of ethics. It has made itself responsible for a profound and irreversible revolution in modern thought, and in doing so has inverted a number of perspectives. One of the most basic things it has taught us is that the best of conscious intentions are a far from sufficient condition for the promotion of right action. Such, of course, was already quite well known to the Greek tragedians, who indeed can be said to have found their only subject in the evils performed by men of good intentions; Oedipus is a good example. We can also recall a passage from St. Paul's *Epistle to the Romans* (7:19): "For the good that I would I do not; but the evil which I would not, that I do." But it was only with the formulation of the hypothesis of the unconscious that this paradox received a stable, psychological, and not simply metaphysical model of explanation. The analyst, in short, has a professional as well as an ethical duty not to remain content with good intentions. We analysts have to be suspicious of our moral rules and principles of conduct up until the moment in which we can evaluate their final and actual effects.

With this as my premise, my reflections first touch on a meandering of general ethics in which the specific ethics of analysis can also go astray. The second group of reflections, on the other hand, addresses an area that lies within the interior of the ethics of analysis; it attempts to deal with the even more specific question of the ethics of training analysis, which of course should be absolutely exemplary.

I

My first consideration is concerned with the leverage of "Darwinian" ethics. The term is, of course, anomalous and has to be placed between quotation marks since Darwin studied the origin of species and had nothing to do with drawing distinctions between right and not-right action. But we are often insufficiently aware of the range and power of the law of the survival of the fittest—the "law of the winner"—which is what we'll refer to as Darwinian ethics. To refer to such a thing as a "law" is itself, normally, to make use of a metaphor, since we presume that no one would ever have imagined any such principle to be right; we imagine ourselves to be faced with nothing more than a cruel "law of nature," or with "the facts of life"—*de facto* law—to which civilization replies with the contrasting notion of "inalienable human rights"—*de jure* law—which would constitute the focus of any system of ethics that can make a legitimate claim to such a name.

But the truth is somewhat different. The classical world, which we admiringly continue to indicate as the source of the whole of Western civilization, was controlled by a religious system of ethics that was virtually destitute of positive values. This is to say, it foresaw a series of prohibitions but prescribed no code of proper action and surely envisioned no such thing as a respect for the rights or merits of one's neighbor. Our "neighbor," we do well to remember, is a Christian invention; and even with Christianity one could simply and easily presume that one's neighbors could be numbered without including women, slaves, or people of color, thus effectively expelling such persons from the province of ethics true and proper and assuring their continued submission, until virtually the day before yesterday, to the sway of Darwin's law.

In the world of ancient Greece, events or factual occurrences, no matter how unjust, were respected not only out of habit or out of deference to natural law; they were revered as a question of faith. Destiny, rather than the will of the gods, was the highest law; and even the will of the gods was subject to it.

Compassion is one of the many profound feelings that Homer shared with the present-day world, but he wasn't bothered by thoughts of justice or by any notions of inalienable rights. Rights were dictated by the whim of destiny; guilt and shame were synonymous with having been abandoned by fate. Odysseus, in the course of his wanderings, encountered Eolus, who was a powerful and beneficent figure: he was the lord of the winds, and they owed him obedience. Odysseus was attempting to find his way back home to Ithaca, and Eolus made him the generous gift of a wineskin in which he had closed up all the storms and hurricanes. The only wind that was free to blow was a mild and favorable

Zephyr. Odysseus sailed to the shores of his homeland within a matter of days, and it was only on having seen them that he allowed himself a brief and much merited sleep. But his companions' curiosity then led them to open the wineskin: the tempests escaped and rapidly drove the boat back to where it had come from, all the way back to the palace of Eolus, who again received Odysseus and his crew quite kindly. But then Odysseus informed him of the reason for their return, the howls that Eolus unleashed were uncontainable. We might expect him to have inveighed against Odysseus's foolish and disobedient companions, but no such thing was even to cross his mind. Rather than being shocked by their behavior, the king of the winds was aghast at their misfortune: "Depart at once from my reign, thou most opprobrious amongst the living. How might I dare to offer assistance to a man who has fallen out of favor with the gods?" (*Odyssey* X.1–75).

Herodotus thought in similar ways. When he describes the adventures of Polycrates, the wealthy and fortunate lord of the island of Samos, he flanks him with Amasis, the wise king of Egypt, who is clearly the voice of the historian's own point of view. Amasis wrote to his friend Polycrates, "It is pleasant to learn of the well-being of a friend and ally. But I like not these great successes of yours; for I know how jealous are the gods; and I do in some sort desire for myself and my friends a mingling of prosperity and mishap, and a life of weal and woe thus checkered, rather than unbroken good fortune. Therefore . . . consider what you deem most precious and what you will most grieve to lose, and cast it away . . . strive to mend the matter as I have counseled you." Polycrates could see that he had received good advice and set out to sea in a ship, for the purpose of throwing his most precious ring into the waves. But a few days later a fisherman appeared at the door of his palace and made him a gift of a great and extraordinary fish that he had caught in his nets. As the fish was being prepared by Polycrates' cooks, they discovered the ring in its belly. On hearing of this turn of events, Amasis was forced to recognize the impossibility of delivering another man from his destiny, and he therefore sent a messenger to Samos to declare his repudiation of the sacred link of friendship and hospitality that tied him to Polycrates . . . "with this intent, that when some great and terrible mishap would surely overtake Polycrates, he himself might not have to grieve his heart for a friend." Shortly afterwards, Polycrates was murdered in a way so cruel that Herodotus refuses to describe it (Herodotus, *History* III.39–126).

So the father of history saw good or evil intentions as having nothing at all to do with the workings of justice. Justice lay in the facts themselves, and thus in a realm of pure objectivity free of all relationship to the will of the individual subject. Herodotus fully recognizes that Polycrates had acted as a just man by following the just counsel of Amasis. But we read on the bottom line that justice lies only in the facts that actually occur, no matter how cruel and absurd. Polycrates is a loser. As a victim, he can merit our sympathy, but not our solidarity; and surely he can make no claim to any other rights than the justice which already has run its course and found completion in the alternation of good and evil fortune.

We know that a society's most radical and profound convictions certainly make no rush to move in accordance with the official adoption of a new law or a new theology. We know that the passage of whole generations for centuries or millennia may not be enough to effect their transformation, since some ungraspable part of them—which we refer to as archetypal more because we feel its force than for having perceived it directly—seems to subtract itself from all the oscillations of customs through which it nonetheless finds manifestation. Beneath official structures—even beneath our official Christian structures—an invincible substructure of myth still largely continues to guide our actions: the myth of the winner, if we tell the story in a naturalistic key; the myth of the favorites of destiny, if we shift our terms towards the metaphysical.

The most visible change that our world has undergone in the course of the centuries lies in our having passed from poor agrarian societies to rich industrial societies. This transformation has been explained in two ways: Marx saw it as having been guided by economic substructures; Weber saw it as having been guided by religious substructures. The first interpretation seems to have been confuted by history, whereas the second seems to fall in line with the views of Jungian psychology: the myth that nourishes capitalism presents itself as a subspecies of a heroic-religious myth that finds its highest expression in the Protestant ethic, and most particularly in Calvinism (Weber 1904). But a question has to be raised about this vision of the entrepreneur whose success in the world of actuality reveals his predilection in the eyes of God. Do we see this vision as a manifestation of a purely Christian ethic, or as a survivor of the ancient Greek ethic that allows no questions on the justice of events themselves, or as an instance of the Darwinian law of natural selection through the survival of the fittest? We can even ask if Hegel and Nietzsche, who supply the roots for such vast areas of modern philosophy, and thus of the systems of education enjoyed by our society's more cultivated classes, find their point of departure exclusively in Christianity. Perhaps they as well are indebted to a more ancient system of values.

These thoughts break little new ground, and one might wonder what they have to do with the ethics of analysis. But they are far from beside the point. They force us to ask if our code of professional ethics actually evaluates an analyst's conduct as good or bad in the absolute, or if instead it supplants evaluation with an act that mainly informs us as to whether or not our conduct has proved to be successful—as to whether or not it has managed to impose itself as a "winning" or "victorious" mode of conduct, or as a mode of conduct that can effectively function and survive in the world of facts. In other words, to what extent within our code of ethics does the Christian tradition cohabit with the Darwinian tradition?

Let's take the banal example of an analyst who makes a gesture of seduction towards a patient: do we condemn such a gesture in any and every case, or according to its factual repercussions? At this point, I can imagine a general reply that would tell me that the ethical code of analysis must set itself the goal of condemning every action that contrasts with its system of values, and not certainly not of offering rewards for cunning; and that only after respecting this axiom should cases be considered one by one. All reports of faulty conduct are first of all to be thoroughly and impartially investigated, and distinctions can then be drawn in some subsequent moment. In terms such as these, the problem seems to present itself, by analogy, as a simple extension of police and penal court procedures: a theft is declared, an inquiry is set into motion, and the appropriate articles of the law are then duly applied.

But a theft presents a situation in which the crime and the interested parties are subject to no great number of ambiguities, and the victim will have little interest in avoiding or delaying the declaration of the facts that have taken place. Calling the police and making a complaint already constitutes a first and elementary step towards seeing justice objectively done. A man who runs a fruit stand can decide that he won't take action against a beggar who has stolen an apple and yet be entirely implacable in proceeding against the hijacker who makes off with a fully loaded truck of merchandise. The margin of discretion that we allow him to exercise in declaring and persecuting a crime can in no way be mistaken for a way of rewarding the culprit of whom he has been the victim: it makes no concession to any ethic of the stronger, of the more cunning, of the successful survivor, or of fortune's favorite. It's quite the other way around: if only we manage to catch him, a felon will pay for his crime more heavily than a person who commits a misdemeanor.

In the ethics of analysis, things stand differently. I am not really raising any question about the possible problem of determining which of the interested parties is the subject or the object of a lapse of ethical behavior. It remains quite clear that analytical psychology considers the therapist no less than the patient to be in analysis, and that the patient too is a subject and no simple object on which we work; but whatever responsibilities we attribute to the latter do nothing to diminish those of the former, whose training in the very theory of analysis should in any case confer a lively awareness of the ways in which these roles are reciprocally intertwined. What interests me here is the risk, and often the virtual certainty, of witnessing the application of an ethic of success, perhaps in some new and refurbished edition of itself, attired in classical myth or Weberian sociology, but no less cruel and implacable than the Darwinian "ethics of the winner." The more able, or cunning, or simply more polished and practiced seducer of patients has fewer probabilities of being unmasked than the inept, clumsy, or perhaps one-time culprit. This, at least, is the conclusion I have reached on the basis of my own experience in the part of the world in which I work. I have sometimes seen cases in which the activities of expert and habitual seducers have finally been censured not because of their having been caught red-handed, but as a result of the discovery of other kinds of infractions that a growing and ever more careless sense of impunity had induced to them commit. The Greeks examined such occurrences with enormous psychological finesse and declared that great malefactors encountered the punishment of destiny not for their practice of good or evil actions (which were abstractions or relative categories in which they didn't believe) but for having given in to *hubris*: arrogance, desiring too much, the knowledge and recognition of no limits. If it were possible to couch that concept in modern words and to define its dynamics in analytic terms, we might very well find ourselves in possession of the ethical parameter which today we continue to lack, and which quantitative formulas are unable to supply. It strikes me that the analysts whom time will prove to be truly dishonest—aside from the issues and polemics of any particular moment—are those who are possessed with *hubris*.

Perhaps these thoughts appear too general, so let me offer another example, quite specific and I think quite illuminating. It's an Italian story, and Italy continues to nourish an ancient wisdom that has led to the lapse of many of the registers of shame: but not the shame of predictability. A tradition of creativity insists on the virtues of constant originality, even in the arts of transgression.

An interesting case in the ethics of analysis—a case quite amply discussed—has concerned an elderly and well-known analyst who was also the chairman of the board of a holding company in which he had led a number of his patients to invest as much money as they could. But of course I am much less interested in any abstract discussion of this analyst's responsibilities than in looking at the concrete role that came to be played by the disciplinary committee of the association to which he belonged. The committee found it necessary to judge the case when several complaints were made, more or less simultaneously. These complaints arose as the holding company was stumbling toward the edge of bankruptcy. But if the imminent failure of the analyst's financial empire was the cause of his analysands' complaints, what does that make of his association's ethical committee? Its statute assigned it the duty of censuring the unethical analyst, but in fact it was called to take action against the incompetent financier! The analyst's punishment derived from his errors in the business world and not from his errors as a therapist. It is in much the same way that I have good reason to believe that unskilled seducers will be immediately exposed, but not their better-versed colleagues.

I find it questionable to be satisfied with saying, well, let's begin by punishing the incompetents, who in any case can boast of no innocence, and then we'll deal with the others as best we can. Situations such as these show little relationship to the case of the theft where one can start by arresting the thief one gets one's hands on and then continue by conducting investigations that should track down the others. As remarked before, the difference with respect to a theft and to the procedures of criminal law lies generally in the fact that precisely the most dangerous offenders can avoid all detection of their conduct, and therefore all investigation.

It follows, then, on the one hand, that our code of ethics has to prohibit the analyst from abusing professional power (in financial, erotic, and all other contexts); but if we are not, on the other hand, to fall into self-contradiction, it must likewise eliminate the possibility that successful concealment of all such abuses be elevated to the status of a final criterion of merit: we would otherwise return to an ethic that gives precedence to factual achievements rather than to rights, or to *de facto* rather than to *de jure* law. It would surely be particularly repugnant for the ethical code of analysis to insist in self-defense on the certain goodness of its principles and intentions in spite of the questionability of the ethical outcomes that ensue from them. We have already remarked that depth psychology has itself revolutionized the field of ethics by making it clear that the guarantee for moral conduct must reside in something other than good intentions. This perception is no less true for groups of persons than it is for individuals, and it has to be part of our thinking about those specific groups of persons to whom we entrust the custody of the ethics of our profession. They have to do more than to work on a basis of just convictions; they have to give proof of having realized justice, effectively and factually.

II

Those who are familiar with Weber's studies of morality will see that we have here introduced another of his distinctions: the distinction between an ethics of principles and convictions (*Gesin-nungsethik*) and an ethics of responsibilities (*Verantwortungsethik*).

It is clear, of course, that ethics has need of both. But real individuals always tend to find their orientation in terms of either the first (convictions) or the second (responsibilities). Those who give precedence to convictions maintain that their fundamental duty is to follow just principles; the rest is entrusted to destiny or left in the hands of God. Those who find their moorings in an ethics of responsibility feel that the faithful observance of principles is of less significance than the concrete and foreseeable consequences of actions.

An ethics of convictions is typical of the Catholic tradition and, especially in Latin countries, of the Marxist ideologies that in fact have redeployed its values in apparently secular terms. Faced with the problem of overpopulation, the Church in no way recedes from its ban on the use of artificial means of contraception. The growth of the masses of the poor and hungry continues to demonstrate that the sexual drive is a great deal stronger than all the prohibitions that seek to contain it (as was already clear in eras that predated Freud considerably), but the Church sees the problem in terms of individuals whom it reputes to be incapable of continence or of the use of the natural methods of contraception, which it considers to be sufficient. Or it chastises governments for being incapable of feeding their populations. An ethics of responsibilities, on the other hand, leads to the study of every form of contraception that might demonstrate an efficacy in preventing the birth of still more people who are destined to a life of hunger. The Catholic tradition has for centuries impressed its seal on every aspect of life in the country in which I live, and this perhaps is the reason why I feel a particular need to lend most of my attention to the ethics of responsibilities.

We can attempt to imagine a few of the ways in which principles and responsibilities, as the opposing poles that inspire our general sense of ethics, can be at odds with one another in the specific case of the ethics of analysis. We have said that our ethical code should impede every abuse of the power conferred by the analyst's professional position (and in technical terms, we are talking about the power that derives from the transference). Such a way of stating the purpose of our code of ethics strikes me as sufficiently generic to allow all of us to agree with it. We are also likely to agree that the formulation of a series of taboos could never do justice to so complex a problem. To declare a total taboo on physical contact with the body of the patient wouldn't be a very wise way of preventing all sexual abuses. Although normal in certain cultures, the lack of a handshake is archaically and inevitably an offense in others, such as my own. To declare a taboo on every monetary transaction between patient and analyst, with the single exception of the payment of professional fees, would be likewise a dubious way of preventing financial exploitation. I have on more than one occasion receiveed a patient whose purse or wallet had just been stolen, so in addition to an interpretation, they also needed a loan to get back home.

When the ethics of convictions encounters the realization that it can't impose such specific and at times humiliating principles, it shifts to a more general tack. It simply proposes to forbid that analyst and patient enter into any personal relationship that lies outside the professional relationship, indicating further that the ban continue for a specified period of time—some would say forever—after the termination of the professional relationship. The specifically professional relationship in fact comes to an end when the analysis reaches its conclusion, whereas no such statement could be made about the transference relationship, which can continue at length or even forever, and this latter is the relationship of which our code ideally forbids the abuse.

In terms such as these, the principle seems sufficiently broad, and, aside from the quantitative problem of the length of time that the interdiction should last, it seems to be something on which all of us can agree—even to the point of allowing us to think that it supplies us with the general law that our profession ought to follow. We seem here to have found the system of rules and rights that can finally assert its precedence with respect to the world of facts. Yet something here is completely out of kilter. For a principle to turn into a law that everyone truly respects, those who debate it and who are ready to propose it must also be able to demonstrate that they themselves adhere to it. And this is something that we cannot do.

The debate on the ethics of analysis takes place within a group of people who have all experienced analysis but primarily in the form of training analysis. And precisely this form of analysis, which ought by definition to be more thorough and complete than any other form of analysis, shows little if any respect for this basic ethical norm. This at least is the case for all the associations of which my knowledge is direct. The transformation of the professional relationship into a personal relationship is, in fact, the rule; and for all relationship to come to an end with the termination of the professional relationship is surely the exception. If transference and countertransference almost always persist beyond the end of a long analysis, this is even more true for training analyses, where it is highly unlikely that the trainer is about to exit forever from the life of the trainee. Quite the contrary, the trainer will continue to be a part of the trainee's life in highly important ways; the role of the teacher in the student's life—as an intellectual authority, as the official representative of an institution, and so forth—will even be reinforced by the termination of formal studies. Trainer and trainee will quite normally become members of the same professional association, and their relationship will gradually assume those attitudes of alliance or diffidence—if not quite of love or hate—that always shape and reflect the activities of our professional institutions. That fact that these attitudes continue to be plagued by numberless phantoms of nonresolved transferences and countertransferences—and that the dynamics of institutional life can make such nonresolved transferences and countertransferences ever more intricate—ranks indeed as a cancer the metastasis of which can kill off even the most vital of analytic societies, but for the moment it is not my task to discuss it. We can likewise make short work of the fantasy that such situations could be avoided by sending student analysts to complete their training in distant associations. Any such procedure would be highly complex and could only, at best, be observed sporadically. The theoretical advisability of insisting on a period of time in which the ex-partners in an analysis abolish all reciprocal relationship seems to me to be recognized for analyses of which the goal is therapeutic, but not for training analyses. It would moreover be far from easy to conceive of circumstances in which any such thing might be possible. The two persons involved might avoid all planned encounter, but the senior analyst remains a public figure who would find it difficult to achieve invisibility: meetings, conventions, and articles continue to present such figures to the eyes of the younger colleagues whom they have trained.

So to center our code of professional ethics on the general prohibition of every contamination of the transference is to run the risk of affirming that in fact we have two systems of ethics: the code of the autocrats (the analysts) who compile the laws without being obliged to observe them; and the code of the commoners (the patients) who have to obey them without having participated in their compilation. Returning to our first distinction, it would again be a question of establishing *de facto* law as superior to *de jure* norms, and our *de facto* law would reconfirm the weakness of the patient and the power of the professional group. For analysts not to feel obliged to apply our own norms to the group that we ourselves form is to make ourselves suspect of collective *hubris*.

Referring on the other hand to the distinction between an ethics of convictions and an ethics of responsibility, I would like to suggest that a thorough respect for our responsibilities could make a decisive contribution to the resolution of the paradox that our profession, once again, seems to place in our hands. We are all *convinced* that the ideal solution is to disallow the superimposition of any and all personal relationships onto the transference; but we are also *forced to perceive* that there are any number of cases in which that ideal remains without realization. Indeed, a series of facts (the reduced size of our analytical associations and, at times, the reduced dimensions of the localities in which we live and work) necessarily impedes its realization. This isn't to say that we have to reject the principle, but surely we have to learn to evaluate the real *responsibilities* that accompany its application. Basically, nothing in analysis can be subject to immediate judgment; it is only with the passage of lengthy periods of time that we find ourselves capable of reaching some kind of evaluation of the infinite intertwining of conscious and unconscious dynamics. When a training analysis takes place between two people who subsequently have to live in close contact with one another in the same professional society, one can be virtually certain that an *ab-use* of the transference will in fact take place (and as well, of course, of the corresponding countertransference). This is to say that the transference—which we have said is highly unlikely suddenly to vanish with the termination of the analysis itself—will come to be used outside (*ab-*) of the natural seat that analysis affords it. It would therefore be revealing and indeed quite crucial, even if no such practice is usually or specifically foreseen by our code of ethics, to observe the ex-partners of the analytical couple after the passage of a few years. The residues of transference and countertransference will surely have been utilized in their relationship—which is to say that there will surely have arisen a contamination between the transference and the personal relationship—but how? Which, if either, of the partners has attempted to make use of it as a source of power and advantage? Have either or both of them assumed responsibility for it? Has the relationship continued to vary in the course of time? Has it abandoned its headwaters and let itself be carried along by the current of the life of our institutions, spinning and scudding in the eddies of professional alliances? Has it shown splashes of collaboration or affection that are more or less ephemeral than such alliances? Or has it slowly consolidated into a respect for individual differences? Replies to such questions, unfortunately, can come only with time. But a time will arrive when we will have to be able to give them an answer, since otherwise we will never be able to evaluate the ethics of those analysts who, in the light of their previous relationship as trainer and trainee, have in any case broken the taboo against the contamination of the transference.

References

Weber, M. 1904. *Sociologie Della Religioue.* Milan, 1982.

Luigi Zoja is a Jungian analyst in Milan, Italy. He is a teacher and training analyst at the C.G. Jung Institute of Zurich and a training analyst at the Centro Italiano di Psicologia Analitica. He is the author of Drugs, Addiction, and Initiation: The Modern Search for Ritual *and* Growth and Guilt: Psychology and the Limits of Development.

Part III

DILEMMA OF THE
ANALYST, THE HEALER,
AND THE COMMUNITY

ANALYSIS:
RITUAL WITHOUT WITNESSES

Fred Plaut

How does it happen that from time to time analysts have sexual relations with their patients, although they are fully aware of the taboo and the consequences of breaking it? The same question could, of course, be asked about doctors and other professionals who are in a privileged position toward their patients or clients. But something special is expected of analysts. I think it is because we treat the patient's soul, and that is regarded as inviolable. This cultural assumption is demonstrated by our attitudes toward brainwashing, which arouse everybody's indignation and incidentally is a tag attached to analysis by its enemies. Even Freud and Jung had, of their own accord, given thought to *suggestion* as a factor in their work (Freud 1916–1917, p. 450; Jung 1958; 1934, par. 315). It is liable to turn up as "undue influence" whenever analysts are accused of malpractice.

Before we can hope to grasp the phenomenon psychologically, we must be clear that any attempt to understand it is liable to be interpreted by fanatic stone-casters as tantamount to condoning it. Remember, the woman taken in adultery sinned by breaking her *marriage* vows, which is not the same thing as an analyst who sleeps with his or her patient. The similarity is limited to sexual misconduct; we may think that her sin was less grave from our sociocultural point of view than that of the analyst. Whether we can be as forgiving as Jesus who, having reminded the stone-casters of their own sins, let her off with a warning ("sin no more," John 8:11) is an altogether different matter, depending on the ethics which are under consideration. Clearly, there need to be sanctions, but the editors and contributors to this book most likely do not believe that punishment alone will be sufficient to have a long-term salutary effect either on the perpetrator or on the society which the punishment is designed to protect.

On the contrary, I believe that noncomprehending action will further darken the already murky background of the puzzling event. If we assume that the men, and more rarely women, in question have often been persons of integrity and good professional standing in other respects, the behavior remains puzzling. If I did not remain puzzled, then I would simply assume that my colleagues acted under a delusion. In that case, I must ask what the image or idea might have been by which they were so deceived as to act as if under a spell.

The King and Queen from the *Rosarium Philosophorum* (Jung 1946, figure 5) comprise an example of an archetypal image that would, if misinterpreted, lead to acting out instead of symbolic realization. The symbol is supposed to represent the incestuous union of brother (King) and sister (Queen) which result in a composite being, the hermaphrodite. But the "incest" depicted herein does not matter as the incest taboo applies to all close blood relations. What *does* matter in the case of analysts is that they are in a special position of privilege. Jungian analysts, in particular, are in danger because under certain circumstances the symbolic capacity of any individual may be lost. Analysts whose private lives are emotionally and sexually unsatisfactory are especially endangered. But this means mistaking the symptom for the cause. Other rationalizations about the pressures that analysts put themselves under when they proudly refer to themselves as "workaholics" could be adduced to explain the disturbed balance of mind of the perpetrators, or that they are "insufficiently analyzed." But when all is said and done, I think that the job of doing nothing but analyzing without the balance of other interests unconnected with the work is simply unhealthy. Job satisfaction depends on an ascetic attitude to the work in all respects, not only sexual.

In an earlier paper, I wrote about the analyst incarnating

the archetype (Plaut 1956). At that time, I had underestimated the fascination and seduction which such images hold compared with our individual consciousness, fragile at the best of times. The symbolic image of the *coniunctio* can deteriorate into intercourse, plain and simple. It is only after it has been acted out that we can see again that a *fascinosum* surrounds the image, which means we must treat it with awe. How could we "forget" about the taboo surrounding incest, *acting as if we were gods and therefore above the law?*

As a first step, I am going to argue that a powerful but unacknowledged ritualistic function is attached to analysis and that this function is a cultural phenomenon which is suppressed by an interpretation of the transference that uses the alchemical picture series as a model but then applies it in terms of individual psychology. I want instead to draw attention to the sociocultural roots and connections of analysis which tend to be ignored by its highly individualistic practitioners (see Plaut 1975). Here I wish to emphasize the role that recognition of the *nodal importance of analysis as a ritual* could play in establishing a basis of analytic ethics. For a start, I suggest that the symbols of union of "the opposites," an abstract term, be interpreted as symbols of "reciprocity in relatedness" to include the individual in her or his culture and society.

But what is a ritual from the depth psychological point of view? In his paper, "Compulsive Actions and the Practice of Religion" (1907), Freud drew attention to the similarity between compulsive neurotic ceremonials and the sacred actions of a religious rite. Acute anxiety was aroused if omissions occurred in the conscientious execution of minute details; the ritual had also to be isolated from all ordinary activities. Freud conceded that there are marked differences between the two and enumerated several. He nevertheless treated the contrast between the private character of the neurotic individual actions and the stereotyped religious ceremonials as merely apparent. In psychoanalytic reality, he found no difference in aim between what he called the "neurotic ceremonial" and the religious rite, or between the compulsive neurosis of the individual and religiosity. He therefore called religion a "universal compulsive neurosis" and felt that the aim and function of religion was partly to repress instinctual drives, the sacrifice of which would further the evolution of culture.

Early on, Jung recognized the deep psychocultural significance of symbols. He saw a fertility rite in the Wachandi ceremony, in which sexual libido is transformed into energy, as available for the sociocultural survival of the tribe (1952, par. 212). Now, if there is a watchword for all analytic schools, it is to bring about *transformation.* Sacrifice is not especially mentioned, possibly because it is in danger of being regarded as a moralistic prejudice. Certainly it would present an unpopular form of ethics in a society that associates therapy with something being done for and to patients, but not by them, particularly if they have to pay out of their own pockets.

However, a greater or lesser sacrifice is bound up with all kinds of transformation. Inasmuch as there is a "before" and "after," transformation involves the crossing of a threshold from one state of being to another, e.g., from childhood to puberty. Desirable as "growing up" appears to a child, there are often twinges of wanting to cling to the previous state, and much more than a twinge when advancing age demands the sacrifice of a previous self-image. Death and rebirth occur several times in one life; a symbolic understanding helps the individual negotiate such crisis points. The body-based self will determine the course of such events as birth and death, puberty and aging processes, anyhow, but the ritualistic enactment of symbols, even the celebration of the new year and birthdays, is a preparation for the inevitable end. Other rituals are designed for the renewal of life at times which are not geared to obvious biologic rhythms, such as baptism, seasonal celebrations, mourning—and analysis.

Analysis has acquired the status and function of a ritual aimed at transformations and ultimately of the renewal of life, both spiritual and psychological. The relations between a culture and its ritual seems to me reciprocal and dynamic: the culture itself is continually maintained by the very rituals that it has produced. For example, from my knowledge of tribal rituals in Africa, I can think of instances where rituals have changed or fallen into disuse when industrial development forced rural tribal life to undergo violent change. In the West, the rise of analysis coincided with the waning power and influence of institutionalized religion. The practice of analysis can be shown to undergo changes, some of which depend on the socioeconomic climate in which it is practiced (see Plaut 1990).

Ritualistic aspects are found in Jung's description of the first phase of analysis as "confession" and the fourth and last as "transformation" (Jung 1931, par. 122). In addition, Meyer drew attention to "incubation" as ritual (Meyer 1949), and Henderson made observations on initiation in the process of individuation (Henderson 1967). Still more detailed observations concern "changes" in the patient during the analytic session, as with the appearance of symbolic dreams and images or the result of analytic interpretations; these changes may be judged by behavior, subjective statements, or a series of dreams. *But the significant difference between religious rituals and those inherent in analytic practice is the secrecy and exclusiveness of the latter.* The confessional keeps its secrets, too, but its existence and aims are known to the congregation, and all worshipers and believers have experienced it. The same applies to celebration of the Mass, a major rite of transformation by means of transubstantiation. Even with prayers, which can be said in the privacy of one's soul, their *existence* as a means of communication with the deity is common knowledge. The parallel between Jung's first and last stage of analysis and the church ritual appears obvious.

But there is no country in the world with an "analytic community" that has anything like the social status enjoyed by religious institutions. Furthermore, the secrecy of the consulting room does receive additional support from our theoretical orientation, as in Jung's alchemical parallel with the *vas bene clausum*. Personal data are also guaranteed legal protection. All these factors contribute to the social isolation of the analytic couple. The mixture of fear and respect which our profession arouses in the general public may have increased our secretiveness. Also the absence of social grassroots and the contrast with such common sense as makes other professions easily understandable provides a source of suspicion against our own. It is as if ordinary men and women, afraid of the unknown in their midst, wait for us to reveal those weaknesses which would make us known and equal with themselves. Our knowing ourselves to be just that is not enough; counteracting the attribution of being in some way superhuman requires stronger evidence.

We also contribute to the image of being the carriers of an esoteric cult or subculture by having stringent admission and selection procedures in our training. So have many other professions. Although we have excluding criteria, the positive criteria, especially for the upper rungs of our hierarchical ladder, are not nearly as well defined as for academic disciplines. In fact, the criteria appear nebulous and arbitrary when viewed from outside the rules and regulations of our training institutes. All this provides the background as well as the soil in which an esoteric subculture with its own rituals can flourish.

Our rituals of selection and admission are of lesser importance, however, when compared with those pertaining to practice. In addition to the special phasic rituals of analysis already mentioned, we find other attributes which characterize rituals in general, such as regular attendance, the predetermined place and hour, the fixed duration and frequency, and not least of all, the patient's financial contribution which may or may not be understood as sacrifice. Furthermore, each session has rites of entrance and exit. Analysts have also been known to think of each session as having opening, middle, and closing phases (although not during the session). What matters here is that there can be no witnesses to our rituals, either in the form of other persons present and participating or as a widely accepted and definable sociocultural frame of reference.

But can feelings, and sexual feelings in particular, be ritualized through analysis? I think the same answer applies here as applies to prayer. It can be an intensely private matter on the one hand, yet publicly recognized and appreciated (or ridiculed) on the other. The great difference, however, is that a person involved can never be quite sure that the sexual drive will not tear off from its mooring, from the emotional links such as the affections of love, hate, and aggression, and go off on a mindless voyage, regardless of sociocultural or ethical context. This applies in other commonplace settings as well, where the individual feels at liberty to confide in someone and so get away from the tunnel vision which "being in love" with one's analyst or patient imposes. Confessors are necessary witnesses.

Any incarnation or idealization of the healing potential of symbolic images of union, such as the *coniunctio* or the alchemical wedding, is highly dangerous and destructive. I want to offer a parable in which Eros himself suggests that the very thought of making the apparently unique encounter public is a betrayal. And in this metaphor it is, namely of his dictatorial powers. Here is how he had come by such powers at the expense of the mortal analyst. Noticing that the latter's life was in need of renewal every bit as much as that of the patient and that an *abaissement* of awareness had set in, he got ready for action. First thing was to create confusion between the symbolic ritual of unification through *coniunctio* by making it indistinguishable from the incarnation of it by fucking or "nourishment by fellatio." Truth to tell, Eros has something to hide: he does not hesitate to exercise his power in the field we call incestuous love, which frequently implies the abuse of power that the parent has over the child, the analyst over the patient. So the case had to be taken to court. The judge decided that it merited a trial by jury.

Members of the jury are the witnesses to the legal trial; they represent the public or society. The proceedings are the rightful ritual required so that both the accused individual and the law of the land can be heard. The accused (here the analyst) may call for the assistance of an expert witness because it is an open secret that without the expert, the balance of justice would be loaded against the analyst. No matter what the finding of the court may be, even if the judge should exclude the public, the legal criteria of a ritual that establishes a fair balance between society and an individual who ignored its taboos will then have been fulfilled. Our ethics, following a parallel course, would have to remain open to constant negotiation before arriving at a judgment.

The individual case in relation to the archetype and its symbolic expression in rituals must be considered in relation to the prevailing cultural and social norm. This implies that we cannot exclude ourselves as members of the public who can also be called for jury service. We analysts are the products of the society and culture in which we live and practice. Our society, for example, is not outraged by adultery but by stone-casters and brainwashers. Here I am particularly mindful of Jung's statement about the conflict between ethics and sex today as not only a collision between instinctuality and morality but a struggle to give an instinct its rightful place in our lives. Further, "Sexuality has an ancient claim upon the spirit which it once . . . contained within itself" (Jung 1948, par. 107). He added that periods of undervaluation and abnormal overvaluation followed one another. Although this was nearly fifty years ago, it is still true today. I therefore choose to remain puzzled or in doubt about the value of equating our ethics with those of the lawmaker. How can they be on a sound-enough footing to make valid as opposed to merely pragmatic rules and laws? It is therefore essential to keep the channels of communication open between the subculture and the culture. To that end, if in doubt—a very big IF—our own "courts," that is, committees, must adjudicate and acquaint the courts of law with their findings.

The absence of witnesses from analytic rituals of transformation is of the essence for analytic practice. I therefore suggest that it could become an ethical rule and a tradition in every analytic society that members who have the slightest doubt about their relationship with a patient, whether in love or in hate, are bound to consult a colleague and—this is important—not pay a fee for the first and possibly only consultation. The charitable aspect of this arrangement is meant to signify that the regrettable transgression is nevertheless a human failing and does not put the person who recognizes this need beyond the pale. What is more, the procedure and the reasons for it should figure under "ethics" in the training program. As a safeguard for patients, it could become an established practice (ritual) that they be made aware of this from the start, and they should also be told by their analyst that they are free to consult a colleague of their own choosing should they have doubts about the ethics of their case, the only proviso being that they must inform their present analyst as otherwise this step would undermine the mutual confidence required for analytical work.

References

Freud, S. 1916-1917. Analytical therapy. *SE*, vol. 16. London: Hogarth.

_____. 1907. Compulsive actions and practice of religion. *SE*, vol. 9. London: Hogarth.

Henderson, J. B. 1967. *Thresholds of Initiation*. Middletown, Conn.: Wesleyan University Press.

Jung, C. G. 1931. Problems of modern psychotherapy. *CW* 16:53–75. Princeton, N.J.: Princeton University Press, 1966.

_____. 1934. The practical use of dream analysis. *CW* 16:139–162. Princeton, N.J.: Princeton University Press, 1966.

_____. 1946. Psychology of the transference. *CW* 16:163–326. Princeton, N.J.: Princeton University Press, 1966.

_____. 1948. On psychic energy. *CW* 8:3–66. Princeton, N.J.: Princeton University Press, 1969.

_____. 1952. *Symbols of Transformation. CW*, vol. 5. Princeton, N.J.: Princeton University Press, 1956.

_____. 1958. The transcendent function. *CW* 8:67–91. Princeton, N.J.: Princeton University Press, 1969.

Meyer, C. A. 1949. *Antike Incubation und moderne Psychotherapie.* Zurich: Rascher.

Plaut, A. 1956. The transference in analytical psychology. *British Journal of Medical Psychology* 35(3):301.

_____. 1975. Where have all the rituals gone? *Journal of Analytical Psychology* 20(1):3.

_____. 1990. The presence of the third: Intrusive factors in analysis. *Journal of Analytical Psychology* 35(3):301.

Fred Plaut*, M.B., B.Ch., D.P.M., is a training analyst for the Society of Analytical Psychology in London and has a private practice in Berlin. He is the author of numerous articles and the book* Analysis Analysed: When the Map Becomes the Territory.

ETHICS IN XHOSA HEALING

M. Vera Buhrmann and G. S. D. Davis

According to the Chambers dictionary, ethics is the science of morals, that branch of philosophy which is concerned with human character and conduct, and it relates to morality and duty.

One of us (M.V.B.) has intimate knowledge of one subgroup of the large Nguni tribe, the Xhosa people, living in southeastern parts of South Africa. Living in a multicultural country such as this one, it is necessary to listen with respect to the psyche as it finds expression in the helping and healing practices of different cultures. We must listen not only with respect but also with knowledge and understanding about other cultures' cosmologies, otherwise there is a strong tendency to see symbolic attitudes and behavior as superstitious or irrational and therefore to be shrugged off and dismissed. Had it not been for my training as an analytical psychologist, I would not have been able to enter the inner world of the Xhosa and make sense of their healing and training methods. Their procedures are highly symbolic and demonstrate complete trust in the unconscious, as experienced in dreams, omens, good and bad events, day-to-day living, and disease as experienced in their bodies.

They are more holistic in the way they experience life than their Westernized countrymen. This was clearly expressed by a Zulu, a Western-trained medical doctor, when he said:

Whites have failed to see that in Africa a human being is an entity, and not in the first instance divided into various sections such
as the physical body, the soul, and the spirit. When a Zulu
(Nguni tribe) is sick, it is the whole man that is sick, his physical
as well as his spiritual being that which is affected. (Berglund
1976, p. 92)

Ethics in Western psychotherapy and analysis have always
assumed an important role in the relationship between therapist
and client, which is intimate and confidential. Boundaries are to be
respected and adhered to. Like the alchemical vessel, the containing boundary may not be broken, and there are also internal
boundaries which must be recognized and respected. The client
should gradually develop complete trust in the therapist if satisfac-
tory progress toward healing is to be made. The development of
this unique relationship can make great demands on client and
therapist, and it is the duty of the analyst/therapist to attend to
boundaries and other aspects of ethical behavior.

This Eurocentric ethical code is not directly applicable to
the indigenous healers of Africa because the setting and methods
of their healing are very different. In working with the Xhosa
group, which practices in a rural area in the Ciskei, it was necessary to divest oneself as much as possible of preconceived Western
ideas, attitudes, and prejudices and to approach their healing procedures with an open mind.

Although their therapeutic methods are very different from
those generally practiced in Western countries, some basic ethical
requirements are present albeit in a different form. The alchemical
vessel is still a requirement, even though it may be difficult to recognize. Here, containment consists of strict rules and meticulous attention paid to every detail in the performance of a ritual or ceremony.
Any departure or negligence can detract from its effectiveness.

In the West, there is a large variety of therapeutic schools,
and the same is true of Africa. This particular group of Xhosa can
be described as "ritual specialists"; other groups such as bone
throwers, faith healers, herbalists, and those practicing extraction
methods and exorcism are not included in the following discussion. The word *ritual* comes from an Indo-European root which
means to "fit together"—it involves fitting things together to create

order. This is the core of their treatment and why ritual is so strictly adhered to (Arrien 1993). Such healing groups and others have served many African communities for many centuries (Kiev 1964).

Therapeutic Setting

The effectiveness of the Xhosa methods is due largely to the fact that they are based on cultural attitudes and beliefs and therefore meaningful to all participants. The therapist and patient usually share the same culture, and the symbolism expressed in the methods is also shared in a meaningful way.

Illness, misfortune, and bad luck are usually due to the displeasure of the ancestors or to lack of contact with them. The withdrawal of their protection exposes the individual or family to the power of witches. This is not unlike the assumption made by classical man that sickness was the effect of divine action and could only be cured by a god or other divine action, hence the temple sleep and the healing dream (Meier 1967). In the case of the Xhosa, the course of therapy is directed by dreams coming from the ancestors. They must obey, do their bidding, and in turn communicate with the ancestors by means of a ritual or ceremony. The importance of dreams cannot be overstressed. The chief healer said, "If people do not dream, I cannot treat them." The Xhosa thus really listen to the psyche, and the psyche is in charge of the therapeutic process and the ethical values and standards. A dream from a patient will illustrate several points.

Dream

> There came a voice from Mr. Tiso's (the healer's) house saying that I must go to my father for "the beads." I started to go, and on reaching the house I saw my father's grandmother, who is dead (an ancestor). She said to my father he must do everything for me, this sickness does not belong to me only, it is for the whole family. (Buhrmann 1984)

The father, who was initially very distant, agreed to get involved and the treatment could continue.

The fact that the whole family was involved influenced the boundaries. The alchemical vessel had not been destroyed, rather the boundaries had been expanded to enclose a bigger whole. Each family member had a well-defined role to play from which he could not depart unless it was indicated in a dream or omen. In this case, the father had to provide the white beads for the river ceremony; he had to host the event and his ancestors, and the clan ancestors of the patient's family, had to work with the ancestors of the healer. Thus the collective archetypal layer of the psyche was also included in the therapeutic process. Ceremonies are the means with which the patient and family communicate with the ancestors.

This dynamic constellation of psychic forces is different from that which is experienced in the transference/counter-transference relationship of analysis. The strict confidentiality requirements and ethical boundaries are blurred, if not considered entirely absent. The attendance of members of the extended family and members of the community at the ceremonies renders the whole process very opaque, and this can cast doubt on the presence of boundaries. But boundaries do exist in the strict observance of roles and rules. Ethical behavior is also seen in the withholding of any ceremony from a person who is not ready to be subjected to it. Nobody should be violated or abused.

In this connection it is informative to consider the first contact between healer and patient. The person seeking help for some kind of stress visits the healer accompanied by two or three companions for the *vumisa* or diagnostic session. If at all possible, this is conducted at a sacred space in the homestead, i.e., a space where the ancestors congregate. The healer gets in touch with the ancestors by means of his guiding spirit. The "sick" person is identified, and his need or problem is exposed. Questions from the group are encouraged, and these are put to the ancestors by the healer. He functions as the mouthpiece of the ancestors. It is clear that the whole procedure is open, and there is no room for confidentiality or secrecy. This attitude is typical of all subsequent treatment procedures.

Inflation is counteracted by the fact that the ancestors are in charge. The healers says: "I am only their servant." This "diluted" relationship between therapist and patient does not exclude the development of transference and countertransference feelings,

because without such a bond, transformation of the psyche is hardly imaginable. In some cases the transference was intense, and
these cases seemed to progress very well. The countertransference
was more difficult to assess. Erotic acting out was not observed,
and this was probably due to their symbolic attitude about feelings.
The emphasis right through treatment was to strengthen the bond
with the ancestors, i.e., the archetypal images in the unconscious
and not the person of the healer.

The personal bond was not overlooked, but again the bond
was experienced in a symbolic way, at the level of archetypal
images and not at an ego level. It is enacted also in a ceremony
called the Separation of the Animals (Buhrmann 1984). The animals are theriomorphic forms of the archetypal ancestor complexes
and are explained as follows:

> During treatment but especially during training/treatment our ani-
> mals work together. Some of mine join him/her and of his/her
> join me, but at the end of training at his final ceremony our ani-
> mals must be separated. My animals must return to me and
> his/her back to him/her. We must test his/her animals to see if
> they are strong enough to work independently.

This indicates the symbolic, suprapersonal relationship
which exists between healer and patient or student during the
many years of therapy and/or training, which can last from three to
eight years. It is an indication of the understanding of the ethical
bond experienced between them.

In this ceremony, there is a mock fight between the healer
and the trainee, and those who support each. It is enacted around
the circular hut from which the trainee will practice in the future
and which is a symbol of the Self. His group invariably resists the
onslaught and overcomes the healer's group. The prospective healer now becomes an independent colleague and is treated as such.

There are cases during therapy/training where "our animals
cannot work together," and the patient leaves by mutual agreement. This can be seen as a negative transference reaction. In this
Xhosa group, financial exploitation was not seen, but it is known
to exist widely among traditional healers of all kinds. Instead, the
agreed-on fee was put down in front of the healer at a *vumisa*

before he starts. If at the end of the whole procedure the visitors are not satisfied, for example, if he refuses to give the name of the one who wishes them evil, he returns the money. His attitude is "I don't want to cause strife."

By acting out the erotic transference and countertransference, deeper psychic meaning is lost and transformation of both patient and therapist cannot occur. When the possibility of sex between the healer and patient was raised, the healers in the discussion group were emphatic that they disapproved of it, but admitted that it could happen with "bad and poorly trained healers."

The healing procedure is so open to the family, clan, and neighbors that secrets and secret meetings are difficult to imagine. There is also a strong cultural bias against secrets. They are regarded as evil, related to witchcraft, and it is felt that sooner or later the ancestors will punish one with some sickness or misfortune.

In discussing general aspects of healing, it was said that "it is better for the healer to cry than for his patient to have to." An aspect that was stressed was that of respect: "one will never become a healer if one does not know respect." This included respect for all creation. It was often noticed with what gentleness and respect they handled plant material.

In the final analysis, the personality of the healer was the decisive factor in the ethical conduct of the healing procedures. The ethical attitude of a healer of repute can be summarized by an extract from the Hippocratic Oath:

> I swear by the physician and by Aesculapius to keep the following oath. I will prescribe for the good of my patients and never do harm to anyone. In every house where I come I will enter only for good of my patients, keeping myself far from all intentional ill-doing and all seduction, and especially from the pleasures of love with women or men, be they free or slaves. (from Rutter 1986)

References

Arrien, A. 1993. *The Four-Fold Way.* New York: HarperCollins.

Berglund, A. 1976. *Zulu Thought—Patterns and Symbolism.* London: Hurst & Company.

Buhrmann, M. V. 1984. *Living in Two Worlds.* Cape Town: Human & Rousseau.

Kiev, A. 1964. *Magic, Faith, and Healing.* The Free Press of Glencoe.

Meier, C. A. 1967. *Ancient Incubation and Modern Psychotherapy.* Evanston, Ill.: Northwestern University Press.

Rutter, P. 1986. *Sex in the Forbidden Zone.* New York: Fawcett Crest.

M. Vera Buhrmannm, *M.D., is a Jungian analyst in private practice and a training analyst at the Centre for Jungian Studies in Cape Town, South Africa. She was born in Transvall, grew up among Zulu and Swazi people, trained in London, then returned to teach and start the Vera School for autistic children. She is the author of* Living in Two Worlds, *an account of her research among the indigenous Xhosa healers.*

G. S. D. Davis, *M.D., is a Jungian analyst in Cape Town, South Africa. She was born in Transkei and lived among the Bonwani tribe which is one of the Nguni group. She practiced as a child psychiatrist in Cape Town before training as a Jungian analyst in London. She is a founding member of the Southern African Association of Jungian Analysts.*

HOW TO HANDLE UNETHICAL BEHAVIOR IN AN ETHICAL WAY

Verena Kast

The unethical behavior of a professional colleague must be controlled and must be minimized. This is necessary both for the suffering of the victim and for the credibility of the profession. If one of our colleagues is acting in an unethical way, it hurts the professional body as a whole. It is not only one analyst's private matter; it can wound the whole community of analysts. This might explain why ordinarily we have the tendency to react in a rather undifferentiated way, especially if we have failed to notice the situation while it was occurring. After the fact, we feel that this colleague must be "punished." We want to know "the whole truth," and in the difficult process of fact finding and thinking about sanctions, the ones who have to handle the problem can become unethical themselves.

How, in pursuing unethical behavior, we run the risk of becoming unethical ourselves . . .

In the search for "the truth," we open private areas of the life of a colleague and an analysand to the collective. Very often there are not only the proven facts, which become accessible to almost everyone, but facts mixed up with prejudices and gossip. Those in pursuit of the facts can easily get into the position of a superego who seems to know what would have been the right thing to do, what now has to happen and what has not to happen. In such a case, we can lose human solidarity, an important value in an ethic of relationship. We certainly have to deal with shadow material, as it must be evident that the shadow of the pursuers gets activated as well. Even the most precise ethic code does not substitute for the full assessment of what happened. In the process, the pursuers are snared by their own shadows, problems of envy are constellated, but not always in a conscious way; old problems of rivalry and unresolved transference-countertransference can influence the fact finding.

I think it is naive to believe that all our transference-countertransference problems can be resolved, as we have no way of knowing how far this process goes nor any way to find out. Every past experience of domination or being dominated involving this colleague is reexperienced. Of course, it would be easier if we could simply be conscious about it, but sometimes we do not allow ourselves to become conscious due to a false ideal of health and growth. We imagine, for example, that we have overcome the authority complexes, but real growth means more than that. It means that we are able to see these complexes in ourselves and deal with them effectively.

As a result of the narcissistic irritation caused by the unethical behavior of a colleague and the consequent activation of the shadow, we can lose sight of the real goal during the process of fact finding. In my opinion, the goal would be that the failing colleague see where he or she has failed, which ethical values have been hurt or are in danger as a result of such an action. There should also be a goal for rehabilitation with ideas about how to help the victim overcome the injury. There should be justice for all, and the possibility of continuing in life and in the profession in a new, more conscious and more responsible way, with a renewed awareness of the very personal danger of becoming unethical.

Ethics of Relationship

In Jungian psychology we react, corresponding with our theories, out of an "ethic of individuation." This means that we each must ask ourselves the question, Is my behavior responsible in a given situation or not, and does my behavior fit with my psyche as a whole? But since ethics are the code of accepted values which are shared in a community, they are never a personal matter alone. We have to ask ourselves not just, What should I do in this situation? but also, What should one do in this situation? It is very likely that between these two perspectives there is a conflict. If we act in a more unconscious way from the standpoint of personal responsibility, and if we do not keep enough of the collective ethics code in mind, the "collective" will act, as it must, to bring its standpoint into the situation in order to regain equilibrium. The "ethic of individuation" often lacks an "ethic of relationship." An ethic of relationship would mean that we are considering not only our own process of individuation, but also the impact of our actions on the analysand and on the analyst as well. One of the most important values in an ethic of relationship is that a real relationship be an equal relationship, not one of domination and dominated. Both participants have the right to be valued in such a relationship.

An ethic of relationship asks, What is good for this relationship so that it can continue in an ethical way? It begins from the standpoint that the "I" and the "you" have the same importance in the process of relationship and the same rights. It implies respect for both the "I" and the "you." An ethic of relationship also takes for granted that we might project without knowing it, and that on the unconscious level we can be both infectious and infected. We do not know how far we are infecting each other in our "communal unconscious," but we must consider it as a possibility in relationship. Ethics in relationship means also that we have to consider the special kind of relationship that is analysis. In the analytical relationship, quite often, analysands hand over their "I" to the analyst. It is not only a therapeutic necessity to maintain and respect the "I" of the analysand, it is also an ethical necessity.

In the best case, the ethic of individuation and the ethic of relationship—both in relationship to a general ethics code—form a network and are connected, albeit sometimes in a conflicting way. Ethical behavior then means that we are behaving in a way which does not damage the relationship or the relevant person or ourselves, and which is in accordance with general ethics. If, on the other hand, we insist on the standpoint of individuation alone (which can easily be compensated by grandiosity), we lack the connection with an ethics of relationship. We feel that we know better and that we have to decide for the "less knowing" person, a euphemism for an unrelated, dominating attitude. But we lack also the connection with general ethics, because in our superior position, which is due to compensation, we devalue general ethics. In this case, we act as though we do not have to fulfill rules: we believe that we are the personification of rules, or we have no rules, we create the rules.

We must also ask ourselves whether our theory has aspects which facilitate this kind of unethical behavior. Perhaps this is one of the crucial points in Jungian psychology. It is important for us, in corresponding to the theory, to behave in an individually responsible way. This means that we must not only follow the collective rules; to do so would mean reacting out of an authority complex. If we understand our theory properly, we have to make our decisions considering the tension between "personal ethics" and "collective ethics." Also, we must make decisions in the tension between an ethic of individuation and an ethic of relationship. Whichever we deny then falls into the shadow.

If one of these aspects of ethical behavior is lacking, then the collective must react. In this way, the outer code demonstrates to the offending individual the difference between values. In consequence, a change is possible, but sometimes it is the long way around to reach this goal. Beginning this particular process means that individuals out of the collective have to enter the problem, a problem which is not their own, but which then becomes very much their own. You can't step into shadow stuff without becoming dirty yourself.

How Can We Do It—Practical Reflections

First, the pursuers themselves must keep in mind the ethical triad. They also need to keep in mind that their problem will infect them and possibly cause them to overreact. They have to be very aware of their own anger, which is connected with such "work," because a colleague may have acted in an irresponsible way and in so doing may have damaged the whole community. We spend time which we could put to better use and have hostile reactions toward having to do something that we did not want to do.

Because of the impossible situation, we never really find out what happened but we think we have to. And there are many more reasons for anger. As our shadow is also activated in the situation, any past problems in the relationship with this particular colleague are reactivated.

Perhaps it would be wiser to have colleagues who are not within the particular group deal with the fact finding, people who know neither the colleague in question nor the victim. It is also important that women and men be equally involved in fact finding (when in doubt, more women than men; since men are accused far more frequently than women, perhaps women would be more objective fact finders). This solution, although an expensive one, avoids a lot of trouble in the Jungian societies and saves considerable psychic energy. How the costs are divided must be discussed; I would propose two-thirds for the colleague, if he or she is found to be at fault, and one-third for the society in question.

As in most cases of unethical behavior, the archetypal pattern of aggressor/victim is constellated. It is very possible that people who try to help will also be gripped by this archetypal pattern. The unethical colleague then becomes the victim, the pursuers become the aggressors. In this way, we damage ethical values of relationship, and we can't change the situation. We even establish it for a long time on this level. I think that the way out of this dilemma is to try to create new situations. In this way, we would be ruled by the archetype of the creator rather than the archetypal couple of victim and aggressor.

But what should be created in such a situation?

The colleague involved in unethical behavior should find a new attitude toward both self and the analysand in question and toward ethical dilemmas in general. He or she should be able to see and accept a way to redemption. (E.g., the colleague could ask the fact-finding committee to find an appropriate analyst for the analysand in question. The failing analyst has to pay for the analysis for the analysand working through the critical issue. Or both the colleague and the analysand could go together to an analyst to work through the critical points.)

But how can we influence a colleague in this way? If he or

she is reacting in an unethical way and is pursued, that analyst will do almost anything not to lose face. Additionally, when people are acting in the dominating/dominated mode, they have narcissistic problems, which means that a way has to be found to build good-enough self-esteem until the analyst is psychologically able to accept the mistake and change attitudes.

We have a chance to achieve this if we can find a way to avoid the aggressor/victim trap. This means that we must clearly separate the team that does the fact finding from the ethical commission. The fact-finding team not only has to find out what went wrong in the relationship but also believe that their colleague can be convinced to return to the ethical values of the society. The unethical analyst should be made conscious of the devastation that is caused to the values themselves. The analyst also needs an opportunity to explain the unethical behavior. He or she should also be made conscious of the possibilities for rehabilitation, because the values of regaining professional dignity and of remaining a part of the professional body could help. After this process, the ethics committee could decide on any sanctions. These sanctions should never be more than what civil law would allow. If, however, it is not possible to show our colleagues that their values differ too much from the values of the society, then our only option may be to exclude them from our societies.

Conclusion

It is very difficult to handle unethical behavior in an ethical way. As we become increasingly conscious of the difficulties, they may become less and less problematic. As a general rule, it is well to remember that in the prosecution of the unethical behavior, we want to create less damage to values than the unethically acting colleague. It does not help to paralyze people or to kill their spontaneity and creativity. I do not think that more and more elaborate codes of ethics help the situation. It would be more helpful if we could create an atmosphere among us in which it is possible to share in an open way our ethical problems and how we have handled them, both now and in the past. In an atmosphere of respect and trust, every colleague may then do the best he or she can.

Verena Kast *is a professor of psychology at the University of Zurich and a training analyst and lecturer at the C. G. Jung Institute of Zurich. She lectures throughout the world and is the author of numerous books on psychological issues, including* The Dynamics of Symbols, Fundamentals of Jungian Psychology, Imagination as Space of Freedom, Growth through Emotions, Interpretation of Fairy Tales, The Nature of Loving, *and* The Creative Leap.

AM I MY BROTHER'S KEEPER?

IMPAIRMENT IN THE HEALING PROFESSION

Joseph Wakefield

Am I my brother's keeper? Since Cain and Abel we have wrestled with the question of our responsibilities toward our colleagues. We question whether we are obligated to help them when they have problems or if we are required to intervene when we believe they are impaired. Although we may think they are impaired, they may not agree. How can we protect their patients, students, and the public from their impairment? What are the shadow issues of power, manipulation, and control when we intervene? I use "impairment" to refer to disorder in the therapist's ability to be a therapist. Because of such impairment, the therapist mis-treats the patient. We will consider why healers may become impaired, why they may be blind to their impairment, and our own problems in intervening with them.

I grew up in a family where alcoholism and disordered thinking were a poorly kept family secret. Various uncles, aunts, grandparents, and parents had their problems. These problems were whispered about behind their backs, but rarely was anyone spoken to in a direct way. Direct confrontations, if they occurred at all, came as frustrated outbursts of anger. No one seemed to know how to intervene as an act of love in a way that could heal. At different times, one relative was hospitalized with dementia and another with alcoholism; neither went willingly. The relatives who had them hospitalized became targets of anger from other family members. It was forbidden to reveal family problems to outsiders.

By age fifteen, I was reading books about psychoanalysis, trying to understand emotional illness and its healing. After many twists and turns, a study of psychology led to medical school, psychiatric residency, and analytic training. I was trained in the 1960s, the era of hippies, psychedelic drugs, and free love. Many of my companions training in the healing professions were drawn to "consciousness expansion" the way a moth is drawn to a flame. Three of my companions training in psychiatry committed suicide. I came to realize that those who aspired to heal others were often deeply vulnerable themselves: members of the healing professions are at high risk for becoming impaired, and trying to heal the wounded can be emotionally draining.

With analytic training came a better understanding of the myth of Aesculapius, "wounded healer," which showed an archetypal pattern in which the healer experiences the wound, learns, then brings that understanding to the healing of others. This is also the worldwide pattern of the shaman. The patient's illness must be taken on by the shaman, who knows it because of the experience of being wounded. We have many names for these experiences, e.g., regression, countertransference, projective identification, participation mystique. With depth analysis, both patient and analyst return to the time and place of the wounding. The analyst also knows that place in part from personal experience and, like the shaman, takes in the patient's wound, metabolizes it, and gives it back in a form the patient can receive with healing. If the analyst's wounds are still too raw, too unconscious, then the analyst may try to use the patient to heal his or her own unmet needs for affirmation, comfort, intimacy, sexual gratification, or power.

Unfortunately, healers may try to sooth themselves in ways that are destructive. Alcohol and drug misuse, acting out by exploiting patients, manic defenses manifested as overwork and self-neglect, recurrent depressions, and suicide are all risks of the profession. The same faulty judgment that leads the colleague into self-destructive drug use or boundary transgressions with patients may block the colleague from self-scrutiny. If impaired healers were viewed as a public health problem, then a medical-model intervention could be described within the categories of primary, secondary, and tertiary prevention. Primary prevention would be avoiding the illness. Secondary prevention would be curing the illness when it exists. Tertiary prevention would be reducing the damage caused by incurable illness.

Primary prevention is attempted by efforts to educate members of the healing professions about their vulnerabilities and their responsibility to guard against impairment. Journal and newsletter articles, workshops, seminars, ethics codes, counsel from supervisors, consultants, quality control committees, and malpractice insurance companies all try to get the message across. Members are reminded that practicing while impaired carries the risk of censure, loss of license, malpractice lawsuit, or even civil or criminal conviction. Members are urged to seek consultation before departing from accepted practice guidelines.

Secondary prevention is what is done if a colleague is impaired. In the usual situation, colleagues who are friends point out the problem and urge that assistance be sought. Many organizations have set up committees to help impaired colleagues. Such committees generally take the stance that it is up to the colleague to ask for help, and that they will maintain the confidentiality of information they receive.

Tertiary prevention is what is done if a colleague refuses to recognize impairment or seek assistance for it. Here one encounters strongly felt differences of opinion. The ethics code of the San Francisco Jung Institute, the policy of the American Psychiatric Society, and the regulations of the Texas Medical Practices Act all require reporting of impaired colleagues who are continuing to practice in a manner that is ethically compromised due to an impairment which they cannot or will not overcome voluntarily. Yet I know many who say they would never report a fellow colleague. It is no surprise that a common public perception of professional organizations is that they are more motivated to protect their fellow members from exposure than to protect the public from harm.

It is often difficult for colleagues to recognize when they are impaired, sometimes because of the defense mechanisms of denial and rationalization. A colleague using such defenses may see with clarity the failings of others yet be blind to them personally. A variation of denial is the feeling of being special, where the colleague has the delusion that unique skills and attributes excuse actions that are denied to lesser mortals.

Additionally, some colleagues may know what they are doing is wrong but want to get away with it. We tend to label such colleagues "psychopathic," which may be more an expression of our anger than an explanation. Finally, colleagues may not accept that they are impaired because they may deeply believe their actions are proper. This leads us to why it may be hard to intervene. Who is to define "impaired"? What are the shadow aspects of our so labeling our colleagues?

Our training as healers teaches that we should be empathic, accepting, nonjudgmental. It goes against the grain to pass judgment on a colleague, especially when we know how difficult it is to do therapy. There is an archetypal tension between being the "good mother" and being the "good father." When the Sandinistas seized power in Nicaragua, some of their leaders were Catholic priests. Pope John Paul II forbade them to participate in the revolution, yet they persisted. When the Pope visited Nicaragua, an event covered worldwide via television, he was greeted at the airport by Father Cardinal, Catholic priest and minister in the Sandinista government. Father Cardinal knelt to kiss the papal ring as a sign of devotion. Pope John Paul II snatched his hand away and scolded Father Cardinal for his disobedience. Father Cardinal wept. Afterwards his friends tried to console him, saying, "the Pope was not a good father to you." Father Cardinal replied, "He was a good father to me; he just wasn't a good mother." As members of the healing professions, we prefer to be "good mothers" and find it difficult to be firm as "good fathers." What is called for is to balance the tension between the two polarities, to be nurturing when needed and firm when needed.

There are many reasons for our hesitation if a colleague denies having a problem. Who are we to judge what really goes on in the privacy of another's consulting room? If a patient reports something outrageous, could the patient be imagining it? After all, we in the mental health profession try to help patients who have problems in reality testing. I have had patients develop delusional transferences toward me—perhaps that has happened to my colleague as well.

Even if the patient's description of the sessions seems accurate, it is difficult for us to decide what constitutes an impaired therapy. Consider these attempted therapies: the psychoanalyst might invite a patient to tell sexual fantasies and feelings, including those toward the analyst; or the medication-oriented therapist might prescribe potentially addicting medications, even for a patient with a history of addiction, if the therapist believes the acute symptoms require it. It can be argued that these examples constitute legitimate forms of therapy. Both examples, however, contain the possibility of abuse, where the therapist could exploit the patient in order to fulfill needs for power, control, or sexual or social gratification. When we hear of these events second-hand, it is difficult to assess what is legitimate and what is impaired.

"Let he who is without sin cast the first stone." I often find "micro-impairment" present within myself. Any of the following could serve as examples of possible impairment: seeing one too many patients today and being tired, unable to concentrate as the patient deserved; responding to the patient with an amplification or anecdote which could be for the patient's benefit but could also be showing off, an expression of narcissistic needs; listening to a patient with inner imagery and drifting into one's own complexes instead of staying with the patient. I know I cannot be a perfect analyst. It is a constant struggle to be a "good enough" analyst—harder still to judge another as impaired.

What of the shadow issues of power, manipulation, and control when we intervene with colleagues? I began here with Cain and Abel because their story raises the question of envy and murderous rage towards siblings. We in the helping professions are not immune from envy, hatred, and the impulse to tear down a rival. Colleagues may compete for status or for patients. Competition may occur on the level of competing factions within the community of therapists (e.g., developmentalist vs. archetypalist, trained in Zurich vs. in the United States) or due to more personal animosities. One way of competing is to denigrate the colleague's abilities; what better denigration than to assign the label "impaired"?

Transferences toward the colleague considered impaired

can make it difficult to intervene. Perhaps the colleague is older, admired and loved. In analytic societies, many of the younger members may have been analyzed by the colleague and may still have feelings of idealization toward him or her. Members trained by the colleague may fear they will be "tarred with the same brush" and themselves viewed as flawed if their mentor is flawed. These idealizing transferences can blind the younger members to the impairments of those who trained them. Conversely, the idealizing transference may shift to feelings of rage and retaliation toward their analyst for having failed to be ideal. So the analyst's problems may be ignored or they may cause a savage attack; both reactions are destructive.

If a patient alleges that the therapist is impaired, the therapist may defend by labeling the allegation a sign of mental illness; the patient may be called delusional or otherwise unfit to make judgments. This can occur with ex-patients also, including ex-candidates. It may be very difficult to confront an ex-therapist knowing that the ex-therapist may expose or distort all that has been revealed in the privacy of therapy sessions.

Issues of power and status within the community of therapists may inhibit interventions with an impaired colleague. Some feel, as part of a good old boy system, that they should never criticize a colleague. Therapists who do speak up may be viewed as traitors to the profession. If the impaired therapist is a powerful member of the community and the colleague is a junior member, the therapist who tries to intervene may be attacked or shunned by other members of the community. In our age of litigation, lawsuits may be filed alleging libel, slander, or defamation of character. These are powerful incentives to look the other way if one thinks a colleague may be impaired. The shadow issues of power and manipulation, combined with the doubt of our right or ability to judge who really is impaired, act as powerful inhibitors to intervening with colleagues. We know that the patient who blows the whistle may be labeled delusional, and the colleague who confronts may be viewed as a traitor to the profession. It is a high price to pay. And yet . . . .

What kind of colleague does not intervene when a colleague seems to suffer serious impairment? Are we not obligated as healers to protect our patients from our own and others' impairments? What are we to do? Am I my brother's keeper? The place to start is with ourselves. If the surgeon has the operating room and the minister has the church, those of us who do psychotherapy have our psyches. It requires a constant effort to remain aware of our shadow, our unconscious needs, our vulnerabilities. Reflection and dream work, consultation with peers, even a return to analysis from time to time, may be vital.

If we think a colleague is impaired we need to assess our feelings. We may have blinded ourselves out of loyalty or an idealizing transference. We might be angry because our profession is damaged or because our idealization has been let down. Perhaps we are afraid of retaliation from our colleague. Often it is suggested that we approach impaired colleagues as a friend and try to get them to accept help. I would say that if we feel anger, fear, or blind loyalty that we should first attend to the problem within ourselves. Approaching our colleague with caring, concern, sorrow, and hope may be the thing to do.

When the colleague does not recognize impairment, intervention is much more difficult. Organizations which rely upon their members seeking help voluntarily discover that the persons who are most problematic are the persons who don't think they have problems. An effective way of responding to such colleagues is illustrated by the Travis County Physicians' Health and Rehabilitation Committee. This committee has struggled for years with the problems I describe above and has learned from its mistakes. First, note the committee's name. It does not emphasize impairment or disability, but rather health and rehabilitation. The committee's members consider themselves advocates for their colleagues. Their role is not to judge or punish. They have no records to turn over to licensing boards. They work toward rehabilitation. Before acting, the committee requires good evidence of a physician's impairment. "Good evidence" usually means someone willing to provide written accounts of the problem, with enough detail to establish the concern's validity. Recognizing the risks of competition, envy, and vindictiveness, the committee does not act upon gossip, rumor, or anonymous calls in the night.

Members of the committee (a voluntary group) have regular meetings to come to know and trust each other. The committee intervenes as a group with at least four members present. The committee does not act unless all the members are in agreement with the course of action to be taken. By not acting alone, no committee member is exposed alone to intimidation or retaliation from the colleague or friends. If a committee member feels frightened or angry, the member steps back so that another member can take the lead. The intervention teams are equally balanced between men and women in an effort to reduce gender biases.

Knowing how colleagues in trouble may be blind or defensive about their problems, the committee presents its concerns as clearly as possible. Since a colleague in denial of the problem will not request help, the committee does not wait for the impaired colleague to volunteer. The impaired colleague is told that steps are necessary for rehabilitation. If rehabilitation is refused, then the consequences are spelled out: the concerns may be brought to ethics committees and the state licensing board. If the colleague cooperates in rehabilitation, the committee does not act as a policing agent. Since impairment may be chronic or recurrent, colleagues receiving intervention receive follow-up, sometimes for years.

Intervention as practiced by the Travis County Physicians' Health and Rehabilitation Committee requires a lot of dedication and work. The task is often thankless and sometimes may feel dangerous. In the short run, it seems so much easier to look the other way, to leave our colleagues' problems up to them, to their patients, or to ethics committees and licensing boards. In the longer run, it is worth not turning away. When I was a child, my family didn't know what to do when a member had problems; family members alternated between looking the other way and outbursts of judgmental anger. We in the helping professions can do better than that. We could help the wounded healer within ourselves and within our colleagues. Perhaps we are capable of being our brother's keeper.

Joseph Wakefield, M.D., *is a Jungian analyst and psychiatrist in private practice in Austin, Texas. He is a supervising analyst at the*

Dallas Jung Institute and senior training analyst to the Inter-Regional Society of Jungian Analysts. For the past several years, he has been interested in the psychological aspects of supervision and impairment in the helping professions.

Part IV

BEHIND ETHICS:

ARCHETYPAL
DIMENSIONS

PSYCHE'S PUNISHMENT

HOLDING THE TENSION BETWEEN SPIRIT AND INSTINCT

Manisha Roy

> The conflict between ethics and sex today is not just a collision between instinctuality and morality, but a struggle to give an instinct its rightful place in our lives and to recognize in this instinct a power which seeks expression . . . the spirit senses in sexuality a counterpart equal and indeed akin to itself. For just as the spirit would press sexuality . . . into its service, so sexuality has an ancient claim upon the spirit (Jung 1948, par.107)

While all Jungian analysts uphold what Jung had to say regarding the conflict between ethics and sexuality, or the mutuality between spirit and sex, not all are in agreement about how these tensions are experienced and dealt with in practice. Since publication of Jung's essay, "The Psychology of the Transference" in 1946, a number of works have addressed the specific issue of the sexual relationship between the analyst and the analysand (including Stein 1974, Henderson 1990, Taylor 1982, Zabriskie 1982, Stein and Schwartz-Salant 1984). Nowadays, we openly discuss the value of the archetypal foundation of sexual and erotic transference only when the action is abated or sublimated. So far as we are able to remain in the realm of the archetype and the unconscious, we hope for the gods to bless transformation because of our bravery in fending off the instinct's assault. We are at a loss, however, when an analyst loses to the disastrous claim of the instinct. Instead of invoking the gods to help the lost human out of such a quandary, we become very non-Jungian and judge such an act as an ethical violation, punishing transgressors by collective standards of ethics. We seem unable to hold the tension of instinct and spirit as they lay claim to one another. Instead, we snatch psyche's authority and fall into the collective power complex fed by a system of codified ethics. In the name of protecting the "victim" in the dyad, the patient or analysand, we remain in the power structure of the transference relationship and totally ignore the Eros aspect. The analyst fails to remain in the tension of the conflict. The community fails for the second time by being the judge and not allowing psyche's "punishment" with its singular process of redemption. Papers on the topic of sexual acting out, which focus almost solely on the effects for the patient, rarely retell the experience and its meaning for the analyst.

In this paper, I recount a tale of redemption for a woman who had a sexual relationship with a student/client thirty years her junior. When I asked her permission to tell this profoundly painful story, she agreed because she hoped that her example could show how psyche's punishment makes the ethical judgment irrelevant in the long and tortuous process of transformation.

The woman, whom I shall call Ann, was forty-nine, a high school teacher and counselor, who came to me for analysis following a crisis with a student/client. She had had an affair for three months with the young man, who was nineteen at the time. We had met twelve years before when she had come to me for a brief analysis. We had had a good connection/transference even in that short time, and she was glad to find me again. When Ann arrived for the first hour, I was struck by how young and pretty she still looked. She was single and childless after a brief second marriage, her second husband having left her for another woman six years before.

The young man, Terry, had come to see her about some problems with his incomplete grades on papers and exams. He had been having a hard time concentrating and had begun to drink a bit too much. Terry was a couple of years older than his classmates because his parents had been overseas during his teens. Ann liked him from the beginning. He came from a well-known New England family with pedigree, education, and money. Ann began not only by counseling but also by offering to tutor him in his studies. She mentioned this to the school principal, who had no objections. They met at least twice a week after school at her home. Terry made noticeable progress within a few weeks, and they both decided to continue with the tutoring.

She still remembered the very moment they fell in love. After six months of tutoring, Ann decided Terry could manage on his own. The last evening, Terry brought a bouquet of roses for the teacher, and as he handed them to Ann, she gave him a kiss on the cheek. To her great shock, he immediately grabbed her and kissed her on the mouth. The shock dissolved into incredible pleasure. It seemed totally normal to become lovers. She realized that they had been in love for months. The affair then lasted for three intense months; they were extremely happy, while Ann tried to repress her guilt.

Around the end of the third month, Terry began to feel restless and asked her permission to date girls closer to his age. They had rarely talked about their age difference or any other reality issues. Although saddened by his request, Ann agreed, saying that it would be the natural thing to do. He made a few unsuccessful attempts; each time he came back to her, asking forgiveness for the betrayals. He realized that he could not love anyone as he loved her. Young women of his own age were uninteresting and dull. Ann then became afraid, worried about Terry's total dependence on her. Something in her wanted to push him out, yet she could not bring herself to do so. All this time, Terry showed unusual maturity in keeping their affair secret. Nothing interfered, but Ann became increasingly nervous.

Then one day, over some small pretext, Terry fought with her severely, calling her names. She threw him out. Now the real fear and pain began. She was afraid he would tell the whole world, the school authorities would fire her, and his parents would take her to court on a charge of sexual abuse. She was so miserable that she applied for an early sabbatical for reasons of ill health. The excruciating pain of losing love, combined with the guilt and fear of being exposed and punished, created a confusion that nearly drove her out of her mind. Then the unconscious sent her a precise diagnosis. In a brief dream, Ann heard the word *Ishtar* and saw a pentagonal design.

After this dream, she knew she had to work with a Jungian and discovered that I was back in the country and lived close by. She was relieved and called me. She mentioned the dream before telling me the above story. I felt a shiver go down my spine. I knew that I would have to help her realize the archetypal meaning of the fateful incestuous love, a forbidden world in which she had no choice but to travel. Noticing her curiosity about the symbols in the dream, I suggested that we both do some research on the mythology of Ishtar. The following week, she came with a book in her hand and told me that a friend had sent it to her for her birthday. The title was *Inanna, Queen of Heaven and Earth: Her Stories and Hymns from Sumer.*

Inanna, the powerful goddess of ancient Sumer, was a precursor to Ishtar of the Semites. Ann delved deep into the book to discover that besides being a queen, Inanna stood for sexual love and compassion. She was the ruler, wife, lover, and redeemer. Her journey to the underworld was necessary for her connection to the dark depth which brought death and redemption. In another version, Ann learned how the son-lover must be sacrificed.

My own readings led me to the discovery that the symbol of the pentagram was associated with the goddess Ishtar. When Ann heard that, she suddenly remembered, from the early days of their relationship, Terry giving her a T-shirt with a pentagonal shape drawn on it. She began to see the uncanny connection between her personal life and a world far beyond herself in time, space, and understanding. Her natural interest in literature and philosophy shifted to mythology and prehistory. She tried to forget her pain by immersing herself in reading and analysis.

It was still very painful for her to get over the young man. She wrote him many letters urging him to come back but was terrified to mail them. Her days and nights were filled with his memories. She missed him terribly and talked about him constantly in the hours with me. She also was terrified of being exposed to the school authorities. I listened without judgment and made only a few comments to contain her predicament. She hung in the middle, too paralyzed to act. A few years before, I had had to contain strong emotional feelings for a younger male analysand and had seen the emergence of creative and healing archetypal symbols in both of our psyches (Roy 1991). Without such an experience, I would have been lost and perhaps would have become identified with her pain and shame. I would have lost the perspective I needed to help her to be in the suffering, and I might have wanted to save her from the pain. It was very difficult at times to remain silent, not my usual style.

Meanwhile she continued to despair and to resist the images of sacrifice and death of the son-lover. She feared the literal implications of the event. She had not heard anything from Terry for over five months. In one session, she kept wondering if he were dead; he had a sports car, and he could easily have run off the road. I gently pointed out that she perhaps wanted him to be dead; she vehemently objected, but admitted that it would solve some of the problems, although she would die as well.

Her enthusiasm for mythology began to wane, and she fell into a deep depression following another brief dream in which she saw herself dying slowly after drinking a green potion from a copper goblet. This dream scared her very much. She canceled her next appointment and called me the next week after telling me that she was very ill. She also blamed me for the discussion about death. Now she would be punished with death by poisoning. I tried to tell her that the dream need not mean her physical death but may refer to the slow "death" she had been going through all these months. Nevertheless, I remained concerned.

I respected her wish to stop analysis for awhile. I had to let her be; she needed the descent. Five weeks later, she reappeared looking pale and thin. I felt tremendous sadness and compassion for her. It was the week before Easter. Knowing that she was raised Catholic, I mentioned Lent, the time of mourning for the crucified Christ. She looked off in the distance and told me that the goddess Inanna had to cross eight gates to descend to the underworld so that she could be reborn again.

She wept bitterly throughout the hour and asked, "If I'm supposed to feel all this, why does it hurt so much? Where is the glory and happiness of my resurrection?" I merely said that there were many gates to cross and Easter was still a week away. The next week, she brought me a few crocuses from her garden. She still looked very depressed and tired. She had not mentioned Terry once in these weeks. She also lost interest in her readings. She said little. We just sat together, and sometimes I wept with her.

Gradually, she began to make her own journey to the underworld. She now saw that her unconscious death wish for Terry was actually the conscious need to let go of her love for him. Dreams were rare during this time, but three weeks after Easter she had a long dream, most of which she had forgotten except for a vivid image of a metal disc with a golden head of flames in it. She knew even while dreaming that it was the sun god of the Mithraic mystery. She herself interpreted the dream, saying that now she knew that Terry was well, no matter where he was. She also knew that something in herself had changed.

I told her the story of the initiation of young men in the cult of the Mithraic mystery and a few other stories of initiation from other mythologies and cultures. It was not hard for her to grasp the idea that the young animus within her unconscious had needed the fateful outer encounter for the eventual transformation. She could sense the archetypal meaning of her role as teacher who needed to initiate her inner son-lover. She saw her excruciating suffering as a punishment for acting the role out literally. I could not have said it better myself. I was astounded by the surge of energy in her as her projection was withdrawn.

This case demonstrates the painful journey of transformation of the older and more responsible partner of a therapeutic dyad. Obviously, I have no way of knowing the young man's plight. Perhaps the same gods who guided Ann and myself also guided him in his confusion and pain. The emergence of the sun god symbol in her unconscious must have conditioned his initiation as well. I have no reason to believe otherwise. Ann's painful journey and transformation was not only an individual event, but showed the mysterious archetypal connection between a modern woman's psychological maturation and the transcendence of the mother-son love in human prehistory, so poignantly depicted by the mythology of Inanna and Ishtar.

References

Henderson, J. 1990. *Shadow and Self: Selected Papers in Analytical Psychology*. Wilmette, Ill.: Chiron Publications, pp. 25–45.

Jung, C. G. 1946. The psychology of the transference. In *CW* 16:163–326. Princeton, N.J.: Princeton University Press, 1966.

_____. 1948. On psychic energy. In *CW* 8:3–66. Princeton, N.J.: Princeton University Press, 1969.

Roy, M. 1991. Anger, despair, fear, and love in analytical relationship. In *Paris 1989: Proceedings of the Eleventh International Congress for Analytical Psychology*, M. A. Mattoon, ed. Einsiedeln, Switzerland: Daimon Verlag.

Stein, M., and Schwartz-Salant, N., eds. 1984. *Transference/ Countertransference*. Wilmette, Ill.: Chiron Publications.

Stein, R. 1974. *Incest and Human Love: The Betrayal of the Soul in Psychotherapy*. New York: Penguin Books.

Taylor, C. H. 1982. Sexual intimacy between patient and analyst. *Quadrant* 15(1):47–54.

Wolkstein, D., and S. N. Kramer. 1983. *Inanna, Queen of Heaven and Earth: Her Stories and Hymns from Sumer*. New York: Harper and Row.

Zabriskie, B. 1982. Incest and myrrh: Father-daughter sex in therapy. *Quadrant* 15(2):5–24.

Manisha Roy, *Ph.D., is a Jungian analyst and a trained psychological anthropologist. Originally from India she has taught at various universities in Europe and America. Her book* Bengali Women *(1976, University of Chicago Press) is in its third edition. She has also published numerous articles in both fields and some fiction. She practices in New England.*

THE HANDLESS MAIDEN

ETHICS AS THE TRANSCENDENT FUNCTION

Maria Teresa Rufini

Often in our analytical work we find ourselves facing the problem of professional ethics. It can be a question of our selves, our way of living the analytical field, of our desires, our passions. It can, on the other hand, be a question of others, when it happens that in the confinement of our offices, in the *temenos* of an analysis, we listen to the narration, often very painful, of previous unethical analytical events, in which mutual seduction found a concrete rather than symbolic expression. Even though sexual intimacy between doctor and patient, and in particular, male analyst and female analysand, is certainly more frequent in the ambit of seduction, I would also list other seductions such as those of guru/disciple, father/daughter, father/son, mother/son or daughter, and so on. But above all, perhaps, I would list the more subtle, all-embracing, and powerful seduction between savior and saved, in an analytical context.

The more burning and altogether more precious conflicts connected with our work fall within the area of transference/countertransference. The whole history of depth psychology is born from a situation of transference not understood, Anna O. and Bleuler, Dora and Freud, Sabina Spielrein and Jung, and so forth. A recent study by two German psychoanalysts (Krutzenbichler and Essers 1991) recounts the history of psychoanalysis from the particular point of view of the problem of the desire of the analyst. The book is short but precise and does not take any moralistic position. It is a documentation inviting reflection on certain simple and incontestable statements (as made by Freud): "Every psychoanalytic treatment is an attempt to liberate a repressed love" (Krutzenbichler and Essers 1991) and "If there is a failure in the attempt of the analyst and the analyzed to stage, during the psychoanalytic process, the 'theater of the Ego' (McDougall 1982) in such a way that the love may find liberation, the psychoanalytical treatment fails" (ibid.).

What is to be done when we are faced with situations where others fail and we are appealed to for help? What other seduction can move us, what great image of ours is solicited—that of the judge, the avenger, the priest, or the caring parent? What is to be done for the daughter Myrrha, who is mortally wounded and claims justice (Zabriskie 1982)?

Jung makes a distinction between moral conscience and ethical function. The former he calls "a psychic reaction which one can call *moral* because it always appears when the conscious mind leaves the path of custom, of the *mores*, or suddenly recollects it" (Jung 1958, par. 855). But the creative force of ethos is quite another function and involves man in his totality. "Like all the creative faculties in man, his ethos flows empirically from two sources: from rational consciousness and from the irrational unconscious. It is a special instance of what I have called the transcendent function, which is the discursive cooperation of conscious and unconscious factors, or in theological language, of reason and grace" (ibid.).

Ethics is, in point of fact, a particular case of the transcendent function. It is obvious that an ethical problem deeply touches all those who are involved, including those from whom justice is requested. The transcendent function represents the possibility of passing to a higher level, the "tertium" between incompatible opposites. The accomplishment of this passage is a symbol which appears and takes us by force, neither conscious nor unconscious, a whole of reason and grace. Ethical capacity is hence an achievement, the fruit of suffering and maturation.

An example of this passage can be demonstrated through a fairy tale, one which M. L. von Franz (1972) has discussed as the report of a painful journey, leading to an achievement and transformation which can rightly be defined as ethical. Here again, as in the myth of Myrrha (Zabriskie 1982), we meet a bad, above all distracted, father who does not realize the harm he does to his daughter as he sells her to the evil one.

The Handless Maiden

Once upon a time, there was a miller who had fallen by degrees into great poverty until he had nothing but his mill and a large apple tree. One day when he was going into the forest to cut wood, an old man, whom he had never seen before, stepped up to him and said: "Why do you trouble yourself with cutting wood? I will make you rich if you will promise me what stands behind your mill." The miller thought to himself that it could be nothing but his apple tree; so he said "Yes" and concluded the bargain. The other, however, laughed derisively and said: "After three years, I will come and fetch what belongs to me."

As soon as the miller got home, his wife asked him the origin of the sudden flow of gold which was coming to the house. The miller told her that it came from a man he had met in the forest to whom in return he had promised what stands behind the mill. "For," said the miller, "we can very well spare the great apple tree."

"Ah, my husband," exclaimed his wife, "it is the Evil Spirit whom you have seen. He did not mean the apple tree, but our daughter, who was behind the mill sweeping the yard." (von Franz 1972)

Here is the harm that the father did to his daughter. We could say, perhaps, that it was the question of the abuse of the father or of an analyst toward the analysand. Without thinking for a moment, driven only by his need (his poverty and hence his hunger), he gave his daughter to the evil one. What does this lack of reflection mean? It means that at the time of promising, the unconscious took the upper hand, while he should have borne well in mind his duty as a father of protecting his daughter. Who is the evil one who wanted to take possession of the daughter? Is it perhaps the incestuous desire? Undoubtedly, but that is not all: together with this, there is another meaning to the figure of the evil one. When harm or violence is suffered, the most serious consequence shows itself in our internal world: first, the loss of trust, then annihilation, and last, hate with the intention of revenge. Hate, like envy, is the ruin of our peace, the sign of our lost innocence.

> The miller's daughter was a beautiful and pious maiden and during the three years lived in the fear of God. When the day came for the Evil Spirit to fetch her, she washed herself quite clean and made a circle around herself with chalk so that he could not approach her. In a rage, he said to the miller: "Take her away from all water, that she may not be able to wash herself; else I have no power over her." The miller did so, for he was afraid. But the next morning when the Evil Spirit came, the girl had wept upon her hands so that they were quite clean. He was baffled again and in his anger said to the miller: "Cut off both her hands, or else I cannot obtain her."
>
> The miller was horrified and said: "How can I cut off the hands of my own child?" But the Evil Spirit pressed him saying: "If you do not, you are mine, and I will take you yourself away!" The miller told his daughter what the Evil Spirit had said and asked her to help him in his trouble and to forgive him for the wickedness he was about to do her. She replied: "Dear father, do with me what you will—I am your daughter." Her father cut off her hands. For the third time now, the Evil Spirit came. But the maiden had let fall so many tears upon her arms that they were both quite clean. So he was obliged to give her up and thereafter lost all power over her. (von Franz 1972)

The harm is done, all the more serious as the father, having to choose between himself and his daughter, sacrificed his daughter. With the cutting off of the hands, the definite severing of the parental bond takes place. In fact, it is the daughter herself who replies to the father: "Do with me what you will—I am your daughter." It is just this clean cut that frees the daughter from the evil one and from the father. In fact, the fairy tale continues with the departure of the maiden, who refused the father's proposal: "I have received so much good through you, my daughter, that I will care for you most dearly all your life long." It is possible that the father's offer to the mutilated maiden, who would remain eternally daughter in a reparative bond without end, is another attempt by the evil one. But the maiden decides to leave. At this point, the long and sorrowful journey begins, at the end of which we shall see the maiden transformed.

The fairy tale continues: the maiden, with her hands tied behind her back—what a wonderful picture of the impossibility of doing—is accompanied by an angel who helps her in her moments of difficulty. One day, it happens that the king, attracted by the mysterious pilgrim and her poverty, falls in love with her and marries her. In place of the maimed hands, the king gives her hands of silver. The fairy tale could end here; the harm has been repaired. What else could we expect? And yet, the real journey has yet to begin. The king represents the dominant of collective consciousness. The marriage with the king, even though seeming to repair the damage done by the incestuous abuse, says only that the collective consciousness lies on the part of the abused daughter and offers her redemption and love. And yet those silver hands, the precious metal of the feminine, are still a prosthesis, something added in the place of something lost. The evil one is still lying in ambush.

After a year of marriage, the king is obliged to go to war, like all kings who must defend and extend the borders of their kingdoms (of the collective consciousness of which they are the dominants). The young bride is pregnant, a sign that her natural creativity had emerged unharmed from the incestuous relationship with her father. But it is just at this point that the young girl is again alone. The king entrusts her to his mother, exhorting her to take care of her. The king's mother is the second figure of mother; the first mother at the beginning of the tale could only weep and show the miller the terrible bargain he had made with the evil one. In the constellation of the young girl, there is a weak, insecure mother, incapable of protecting her daughter.

The king's mother does not appear to be bad. It could be said that this type of mother prevails in a patriarchal culture. But the weakness of the second mother offers the evil one another opportunity to take possession of his longed-for prey. On the birth of the baby, the queen mother sends the happy news to the king, and he, happy in his turn, replies telling her to take care of the baby until his return. The evil one intervenes: while the messenger is asleep (the nonvigilant consciousness, an open space for the eruption of the unconscious), the evil one changes the king's letter to an order of death for the newborn child. The queen mother is horrified, but twice more the letters are exchanged and changed by the evil one. Now this second maternal figure finds the only way of salvation for the young daughter-in-law and the baby: flight and secrecy. And, in fact, how can such a terrible figure, the evil one, be opposed in any other way? Does not this way of patience recall the attitude of Job, as commented on by Jung in "Answer to Job" (1952)?

The young girl therefore resumes her journey. After the first separation from the original family, this second departure is necessary in order to further her individuation process. Now she takes three additional things with her: the baby—her creative capacity; being a queen—having been loved and chosen by the king by reason of her mutilation; and the silver hands—signs of love and reparation at a wholly human level. The young queen in flight "weeping bitterly, soon entered a large forest and there she fell upon her knees and prayed to God." An angel approached her and led her to a small house, "over the door of which was a shield inscribed with the words: 'Here may everyone live freely.'" The queen spent seven years in this small house "and was well cared for; through God's mercy on her, on account of her piety, her hands grew again as before."

The seven years spent in the house, the loving presence of a feminine figure, "a snow-white maiden," indicate a time of deep introversion for seeking the feminine values which had been abused. These then rekindled the desire of the evil one. Seven years represent a cyclical time, a period of initiation, an allusion to the lunar period connected with the feminine. In these seven years, we can imagine that the young girl finally could be in touch with a feminine world and not so easily prey to the whole masculine world—the object of desire, of carelessness, in the end saved only on account of her poverty and endurance of suffering—but a feminine world full of autonomy and force, once again capable of its creativity—the hands which grew again "on account of her piety."

However, the journey still cannot be considered complete.

Must we perhaps imagine that for the young queen there is no longer the possibility of encounter with the masculine world? It is at this point that the king—back from war, having cleared up with his mother the misunderstanding of the letters, and above all recognizing the work of the evil one—sets out in a desperate search for the young queen. Such is right: even the masculine world cannot but be touched by the events of the feminine and must in turn make its journey, to seek. This is a well-known topic, found in the tale of Amor and Psyche and in Mozart's *The Magic Flute*.

Last, it is worthwhile to dwell upon the encounter of these two lovers. Seven years have passed, years of traveling and fasting, for the king had sworn "Neither will I eat nor drink until I have found my dear wife and child." What does this oath mean? The king has immediately perceived in natural impulse, i.e., hunger, thirst, and sexuality, something which must be sacrificed to be able to find the fugitive queen and rebuild the pair, not only on a natural but also on a symbolic level. After seven years, the king reaches the house in the forest. An angel receives him and offers him food and drink, but the king refuses and "lay down to sleep and covered his face with a napkin." In this sleep of the king, but above all in his face covered by the veil, we find the last mysterious step in his symbolic quest, the hiatus between the two levels of consciousness, the giving up of the ego, of its claims—in other words, the defeat of the ego of which Jung speaks, when confronted with archetypal energies. The face covered by a veil takes us back to the rituals of initiation, to the time of silence and symbolic death.

Only at this point can the two find each other again. The baby is now seven and does not know his father. The king does not recognize the wife, he is doubtful: "My wife had silver hands," he says. The queen, who is the only one without doubt, shows the king the silver hands she had kept in the house. Great is the joy at the happy conclusion. The tale ends in a significant manner: "After eating a meal together with the angel, they went home to the king's mother." Finally, the king can eat again and can again resume the naturalness of this desire. Once they have returned to their kingdom, "their arrival caused great rejoicing everywhere; and the King and Queen celebrated their marriage again and lived happily together until the end of their lives." The marriage is thus celebrated a second time, to signify the deep transformation of the couple.

What has all this to do with the ethical function? The very fact that the reader may pose this question shows that on reflection we have moved to a more complex consideration of the whole event. At the beginning, it is possible to criticize the father bitterly, as he was guilty of giving his daughter to the evil one, first through inattention and then out of fear and to save himself. And where was the mother, we have perhaps asked ourselves, trying to find someone to blame. The mother was also unable to protect her daughter by inventing something, perhaps, or by offering herself in exchange. Would we not be inclined also to blame the evil one, always ready to take possession of our soul? The events of the tale show us instead that, once hurt, the only road that lies open to us is that of descending into ourselves, to recompense the balance broken by the eruption of evil. Not revenge, but sorrow; not hatred, which inseparably binds us to whomever abused us, but detachment and silence.

What happened to the father and to the evil one at the end of this tale? We know nothing more, and perhaps we are not interested. The father has disappeared. The evil one has had to give up his intention. More importantly, the young girl regained her hands and is now able to have a happy and constructive relationship with the king, whether he represents her real companion or her creative animus; and above all, she has her son with her, born in accordance with the natural and unknowing order of the collective consciousness, the son who, after seven years of pain and silence, has finally known his father and been recognized by him. We could now imagine this young girl as a strong woman, who did not sit aside weeping but had the courage to bear her pain and her tears and, without hate, traveled along her own road.

References

Krutzenbichler, H. S., and H. Essers. 1991. *Muss denn Liebe Sunde sein? Uber das Begehren des Analytikers.* Freiburg: Verlag Traute Hensch.

Jung, C. G. 1958. A psychological view of conscience. In *CW* 10:437–455. Princeton, N.J.: Princeton University Press, 1964.

_____. 1952. Answer to Job.In *CW* 11:355–472. Princeton, N.J.: Princeton University Press, 1969.

von Franz, M.-L. 1972. *The Feminine in Fairy Tales*. New York: Spring Publications.

Zabriskie, B. 1982. Incest and myrrh: Father-daughter sex in therapy. *Quadrant* 15(2):5–24.

Maria Teresa Rufini *is a Jungian analyst in Rome, Italy, and a training analyst for the Associazione Italiana di Psicologia Analitica. With a doctorate in philosophy, classical literature, and psychology, she has a special interest in myth, fairy tales, and symbols.*

TRANSFERENCE-COUNTERTRANSFERENCE

THE EROS-AGAPE FACTOR

Rosemary Gordon

The basic ethical ideas of doctors or analysts are, or so it seems to me, simple and straightforward. After all, they have chosen their profession because of an internal drive, or even command, to help or heal the "other," their own welfare and satisfactions having been relegated as secondary to or even dependent on the welfare of the patient. However, the healing of the psyche, we now know, is infinitely baffling and complex; it involves no extraneous instruments or mechanisms but is effected by that which partakes of its own nature, that is, the psyche of the doctor or analyst. Consequently, the study of the therapeutic process depends on an ever-evolving, never-ceasing exploration, not only of the psyche of the patient but also of the psyche of the doctor or analyst as well as the interactions of the psyches of the two.

This is neither a new discovery nor a new understanding. Both Freud and Jung quite early on speculated about the processes involved in the art of healing the psyche. Freud, for example, in his lectures to the physicians recognized the depth of involvement of the doctor's psyche when concerned with the therapy of a patient, for he suggested that "in the analytic process the doctor must bend his own unconscious like a receptive organ towards the emerging unconscious of the patient" (Freud 1912). In other words, Freud knew then that analysis involved the strange interaction of two persons. Unfortunately, this early awareness was not really pursued by Freud and his followers until many years later.

Jung, however, did carry these ideas further when he suggested to Freud that all who would be analysts must first undergo a personal analysis, an idea which Freud did in fact accept. Jung recognized that in the work of analysis very personal forces are released between patient and analyst, forces of such great intensity that he compared this process to the combination of two chemical substances: "For two personalities to meet is like mixing two different chemical substances; if there is any combination at all both are transformed" (Jung 1931, par. 163). Jung also acknowledged that there is what he called the "demon of sickness" provoking psychic infection, for the patient can transmit the disease to a healthy person whose powers then subdue the demon; and furthermore that "it is futile for the doctor to shield himself with a smoke screen of fatherly and professional authority" (ibid.).

However Jung also warned that the doctor or analyst must remain connected to consciousness and maintain a balance between "understanding and knowledge." Failing to retain consciousness, the analyst . . .

> falls into the same dark hole of unconsciousness as the patient, and then instead of the transference-countertransference situation you get "participation" which is characteristic of primitive psychology when there is no longer discrimination between subject and object. (Jung 1968, par. 322)

Thus Jung was aware of the power of the affective unconscious forces that are released in and by the analytic process; he was aware also of the pain, sacrifice, and dangers that this can bring to the doctor-analyst.

I believe that a further insight and discernment of our feelings and transactions with patients might be enhanced by incorporating into our analytical vocabulary the two great Greco-theological concepts of agape and Eros, two names that denote different forms of love (see Lambert 1981). The study of the etymological roots of these terms has a somewhat complex and checkered history. Agape was one of the cult names of Isis. It was not used as a noun in Greece, but only as a verb or adjective when it was used to denote sympathy, mutual respect, and the friendship of equals. Lambert found that in classical Greek agape referred to qualities like:

1. Not seeking one's own advantage.
2. Not being inflated with pride and vanity.
3. Not being envious.
4. Not being vengeful.
5. Caring for the advancement of truth.
6. Being hopeful for all things.

This is surely a good list of the qualities we analysts aim to have and develop.

Eros, on the other hand, was used and discussed by the Greeks more often, more freely, and with more enthusiasm than agape. Eros meant power, magic, ecstasy; it referred to impulse and desire, and attraction to physical beauty. Although it could degenerate into frenzy, in its higher form it could transport man or woman beyond himself or herself. Euripides described the god Eros as "the tyrant over gods and men." Plotinus refers to Eros as "the overwhelming desire for union with the One" (Lambert 1981).

Given the qualities ascribed to agapaic love, this term might indeed be valuable if introduced into the analytic context, for it draws our attention to those attitudes we need to cultivate in relation to our patients. But there is the danger that a list of such desirable qualities could encourage an idealization of the analyst and of his or her role and function. It could encourage the illusion that he or she is invulnerable and free from all defects and all temptations.

It is important that, rather than simply relying on repression, denial, or identification with persona, we analysts remain sufficiently confident that we can manage to control and more or less master our own reactions to patients. In this way, we can avoid acting them out in a hasty, untimely, unconsidered, or self-gratifying way. Or if we have acted out, we can fairly quickly regain consciousness and explore why this happened. We can also find out to what extent our behavior belongs to our own psychopathology—or "countertransference illusion" to use Fordham's term (1976, p. 150). Or if it is part of the patient's inner world, then we are dealing with "countertransference syntony," the unconscious interaction between the analyst and the patient. The latter could be, at least in part, the result of projective identification, what Jung has called "psychic infection." At such times, a repowering of agapaic love could encourage and strengthen the analyst's capacity to listen, to remain hopeful, and to trust that the patient is capable of further development and growth.

But however desirable the presence of agape in the countertransference may be, there is also, I believe, a real need for Eros, whose dynamic force must complement and counterbalance agape. For if there is but little Eros available for investment in the patient-analyst relationship, and if there is a dominance of agape at the expense of Eros, the analytic work is likely to be dull, flat, colorless, and without vitality, passion, and deep mutual involvement. Admittedly, without Eros the analyst and/or the patient may feel very virtuous, pure, and correct. They may feel they are good and doing their duty. But the cost is high, and the possible achievement of an actual transformation of the psyche is extremely limited.

After all, analysis involves a long-term commitment and the passage through many moments of anguish and pain, of love and hate, of resentment and gratitude. All of this could probably not be sustained by either patient or analyst if agape alone were present without Eros. Neither patient nor therapist could or would be willing to accept the risks and the upheavals of their mutual and often deeply unconscious feelings and fantasies and the exposure revealed by the analysis of projection, introjection, and projective identification. All of this demands an enormous amount of effort, work, and pain. Where not just normality, but actual transformation is sought, the transporting power of Eros must be available to come into play. Thus, so I believe, both agape and Eros are essential constituents of an analyst's experience of and love for the patient. But the balance between these two forms of love is bound to vary and shift from person to person and from time to time. It must therefore be assessed and reassessed continuously. We must explore again and again when, how, and in what way an imbalance between them might have produced some particular negative therapeutic situation.

I want now to examine, through some clinical examples, the value and usefulness of thinking in terms of the agape-Eros factor. A patient, whom I will call Joan, had been in a long analysis with a colleague, a woman in late middle age, who died quite unexpectedly and suddenly after a short illness. Joan had loved and admired her analyst. She had felt totally understood by her, felt that they were very much in tune, shared a very similar ethos and ideology and had similar liberated and feminist attitudes. But from what she expressed to me, it seemed as if little work had been done on the defenses and the resistances or on the negative transference feelings or the shadow components of her own or her analyst's personality; yet she remembered that her analyst had sometimes warned her of the dangers of an idealizing transference.

For a few weeks after her analyst's death, Joan thought that she would be able to manage without any further analysis. But then one night she dreamed of her analyst as an evil ghost or witch who had come to haunt or disturb her. When such upsetting and terrifying dreams about her analyst occurred several more times, she felt impelled to seek further analysis, and so came to me.

Joan's feelings about me were for a long time hostile and angry. I was obviously very unsatisfactory compared to her previous analyst, who she was sure loved her deeply, for whom she was quite special, who loved her more than any of her other patients, who could see all her qualities and talents and gifts, and who actually found her very beautiful and sexually attractive and exciting. As I listened to her, it occurred to me that Joan was confusing erotic and agapaic love, and that her perception of her analyst was overburdened with Eros and deficient in a recognition and acknowledgment of agape.

This raises an issue that I have not mentioned or discussed so far, the problem of the agape-Eros balance within the *patient*. The Eros-agape balance is a factor not only in the analyst's feelings and reactions to the patient, but also in the patient's perceptions, reactions, and expectations of the analyst. In Joan's case, this imbalance in her expectations and misinterpretations of her analyst's feelings for her seemed to betray her unconscious longing for her mother's sensuous appreciation of her little girl's body. Her mother, to judge by the way she spoke about her, was a very attractive and sophisticated, but narcissistic, cold and frigid woman, who hardly ever touched and certainly never cuddled Joan. However, she had made Joan feel that there was absolutely no chance that she could ever become as sexually attractive and desirable as her mother. Joan's family was otherwise free and uninhibited, a family in which sex was discussed freely and often. In other words, while erotic love appears to have held the stage in that family and seemed to be, so Joan thought, the predominant relationship in adult life, she herself had little experience of the other, the agapaic love, in her childhood.

Peter Rutter (1989) describes the frequent abuses of women by professional men in a professional relation to them, in his courageous but alarming book. He thus forces us to look even more carefully and deeply at the transference-countertransference process and the powers released in the helper-helped interaction. It encourages us to continue to search for ever more signposts or signals to orient ourselves in relation to our patients.

His description of his own experience with his patient Mia is a sensitive and perceptive account that shows us how easy it is to confuse empathy, sympathy, care, and compassion with one's own erotic impulses and desires. Mia had come into treatment because she tended to become sexually intimate with men easily, often because she felt she had no other way to keep them interested. One day, she seemed without warning to direct her sexuality toward Rutter, her therapist. He experienced this sexual posturing in her behavior as becoming more intense. She looked at him pleadingly, "wondering through her tears" whether men would always use her and then throw her away. She slid from her chair, began to edge toward him, brushing her breasts against his legs; she buried her head in his lap. She was the last patient that day, and they were the only people left in the office building. There had been losses in Rutter's personal life, he had been depressed at that time, and lived alone in "an empty house":

> I was overcome by an intoxicating mixture of the timeless free-
> dom and the timeless danger that a man feels when a forbidden
> woman's sexuality becomes available to him—and very, very vul-
> nerable. From this experience I discovered at first hand just how

passionate and dissolving the erotic atmosphere can become in relationships in which the man holds the power and the woman places trust and hope in him. (Rutter 1989, p. 4)

In that incident, Rutter realized *just in time* how harmful a sexual enactment would have been. But having come so close to it, having at that time allowed himself to experience his own sexual desires and her seductiveness, he was then able to analyze and demonstrate to Mia her particular illness with its ever-repeating compulsive and self-destructive pattern, which left her so often the victim of her many sexual partners.

When Rutter suggests that the illusion of a love created in the "forbidden zone" is almost always entirely the product of a "healing fantasy," is he not pointing also to the possibility of confusing, only too easily, agape and Eros? Indeed, the confusion, or lack of discrimination, between agape and Eros can infect even analytical theorizing. Wilhelm Reich believed that the orgasm itself was therapeutic, that it released creative and energizing forces, and therefore that the analyst or psychotherapist, in order to help and heal the patient, should make love to her (Reich 1983). In other words, he seemed to be confident that the sexual encounter would be a token of his loving concern for the patient. For him agape and Eros seem totally undifferentiated.

Peter Rutter cautioned that a male doctor or analyst could be sexually seductive if he asked a female patient to report to him her sexual feelings about him. Does such a warning imply that a man cannot really analyze a woman patient, for he dare not explore her infantile fantasies? He might be tempted to react to them as though they belonged to the "here and now" and thus fail to recognize them as being a repetition, a reexperiencing of feelings and impulses that stem from her early babyhood or childhood. Of course, one would not actually ask for such particularized fantasies. But surely the analyst must be available to hear them, receive them, and experience his role in relation to them, and yet not act them out.

I wonder if there could be a difference between men and women in terms of a possible imbalance or confusion between Eros and agape, at least in our present day culture? To judge from what I have heard, read, or met with personally, it seems that male analysts have greater difficulty in keeping their sexual responses under control and subjected to the demands of agape. In fact, they seem liable to be excited, fascinated, and almost haunted by their female patients, whose narcissistic and/or oedipal complexes provoke and stimulate their own sexual-erotic impulses and desires. Their patients' transference feelings may indeed mesh with their own unconscious, unresolved longings for mother or anima figures, which may lie in readiness to stir and lead to actual enactment.

In women analysts, the therapeutic process seems to evoke more readily the maternal functions, which are probably closer to agapaic love. Rather than perceiving their patients as alluring or seducing strangers, they are more likely to experience them as children that need caring and watching over. But this may tempt the woman analyst to hold back and so obstruct the development of patients. Unconsciously, the female analyst may not want them to grow up or become adults. They may try to cosset them ever so gently and bewitchingly and keep them close to their metaphorical breasts, so that there remains little wish or incentive in the patient to move out into the open, uncertain, and storm-tossed world.

To conclude and summarize this paper: I have argued that the distinction and differentiation of the Eros and agape factors is a useful and valuable sophistication in an analysis of transference and particularly of countertransference. It helps us to recognize, to understand, and to take into account a further dimension that affects the vicissitudes of the countertransference. The balance between these two opposed but complementary ways of loving is delicate. It needs to be scrutinized and examined constantly and looked at in relation to the needs of the individuals involved. Both forms of love are necessary and both play their part in the powerful yet fragile interaction and interdependence of patient and analyst. When and how much this needs to be discussed and made explicit is something that each situation and each couple must experiment with and work out for themselves.

The distinction and differentiation of the Eros-agape factor could help to transform into something alive, meaningful, and understandable what is otherwise a temptation either to act out or to follow a cold, moralistic, and legalistic rule or code. It will help the analyst to explore and then come to understand and to trust his or her own reactions.

Going back to the discussion of ethics in analysis, it seems to me that this is really identical with the ethics covered by the Hippocratic oath that governs the work and behavior of the medical doctors. But given the enormous complexity of the analytic relationship, this does raise the problem of how to deal with those who have infringed the ethical code. Undoubtedly this will require much thorough exploration and compassion for the persons involved. After all, the analytic stance tends to be on the side, not of punishment, but of furthering psychic growth, evolution, and individuation.

When Christ met those assembled to kill the woman taken in adultery, he argued that only those without sin might throw the first stone; he then averted his eyes, looked at the sand, "stooped down and with his finger wrote on the ground. And they which heard it, being convicted *by their own conscience* went one by one" (John 8:1-11). Rather than setting up a judge and his court on the outside, Jesus encouraged the people to turn inward and develop their own conscience, their own trial and verdict. Is this not a worthwhile example to follow, particularly by analysts?

References

Fordham, M. 1976. *The Self and Autism.* London: William Heinemann Medical Books.

Freud, S. 1912. Recommendations for physicians on the psycho-analytic method of treatment. *SE*, vol. 22. London: Hogarth.

Jung, C. G. 1931. Problems of modern psychotherapy. In *CW* 16:53-75. Princeton, N.J.: Princeton University Press, 1966.

_____. 1968. The Tavistock lectures. In *CW* 19:5-182. Princeton, N.J.: Princeton University Press, 1976.

Lambert, K. 1981. *Analysis, Repair and Individuation.* London: Academic Press.

Reich, W. 1983. *The Function of the Orgasm.* London: Souvenir Press.

Rutter, P. 1989. *Sex in the Forbidden Zone.* Los Angeles: Jeremy P. Tarcher.

Rosemary Gordon, Ph.D., is a Jungian analyst in private practice in London, England. She is a training analyst for the Society of Analytical Psychology and the British Association of Psychotherapists. She is editor of the Journal of Analytical Psychology and author of Dying and Creating: A Search for Meaning and Bridges: Metaphor for Psychic Processes.

THE HEALING CONIUNCTIO AND ITS SEXUAL-ROMANTIC SHADOW

John Steinhelber

It has been terribly disturbing to hear about so many casualties among patients and psychotherapists for whom therapy or analysis has given way to sexual and romantic involvements. To help understand how a therapeutic partnership can be drawn toward a sexual-romantic liaison, and how obeying that attraction can have tragic consequences, we might explore the shadow side of a healing archetypal pattern, thus potentially illuminating not only the shadow but many aspects of that archetype. C. G. Jung found in alchemy a rich collection of symbolism for understanding the archetypal bases of psychological transformation and individuation. His alchemical studies deal extensively with boundaries and unions between psyche and body and thus provide an ideal context for exploring the sexual-romantic shadow of the psyche's healing efforts.

In the concluding section of *Mysterium Coniunctionis*, entitled "The Conjunction," Jung follows the work of Gerard Dorn, a sixteenth-century alchemist, who organized an immense array of alchemical processes into three basic stages. The first stage had two aspects: uniting the spirit and the soul, and separating that unity from the body. The second stage then reunited the spirit-soul with the body, or with an essence within the body. The third stage joined that union with the *unus mundus*, the oneness of the world.

Uniting Spirit with Soul, Separating from the Body

In the first stage, the alchemists attempted to bring a certain order to the original *massa confusa*. This work involved striving to *unite* symbolically the spirit and soul in a *unio mentalis* and, at the same time, to *separate* that spirit-soul union from the unacceptable body, thus overcoming the body's instincts and emotions. The union and separation of stage one had intrinsic value as well as being prerequisites for proceeding further.

Analogously, in the basic work of Jungian therapy, there might be a striving to unite the soul's psychological energy with the spirit or mental qualities of an analytic attitude, coupled with an effort to separate and protect that therapeutic alliance from the dangers of the embodied or outer world. An example of this occurred when, after a year and a half of reasonably effective psychotherapy, a patient announced that he had decided to quit therapy immediately. The hour ended with the therapist and patient unsure that they'd ever meet again. A few days later, the patient phoned to reschedule. When he returned, he explained his impulse to terminate: he had figured out that the therapist, a male, was gay (a fantasy that happened to be incorrect) and expressed fears that the therapist might not understand the patient's heterosexual life, might have "different morals," or "might be too much into your own trip in here."

The patient had been repeatedly abused sexually by older males as a youngster. Referring to that shared knowledge, it was then possible to resume therapy by exploring and appreciating his need to have absolute assurance of the separation of analytic work from bodily dangers, as in alchemy's stage one. At the same time, there was a joining of his soul energy with the spirit or mental quality of analytic exploration. Through that separating and joining of the alchemical first stage, the therapy was able to proceed.

Spirit-soul union and its separation from the body are not always so easily attained. A temptation may arise to eliminate the necessary separation. During "stage one" work in therapy, therapists and patients sometimes find themselves with feelings toward each other which they interpret as "real" attraction and "genuine" romantic love, i.e., not based on therapy-specific projections. They believe that the transference and countertransference have not really heated up yet, and that their romantic love is "real." Sometimes they decide to stop the therapy and begin a sexual-romantic relationship. Alchemically, how do we understand what happens when the participants decide that it is, and needs to be, "real" romantic love?

We might consider two possibilities when this occurs during the first alchemical stage. First, the therapist and patient may not have entered very fully into the alchemical container. With respect to the psychotherapeutic process, their experience of romantic love may be in part an unconscious resistance to the *separation* component of stage one and if lived out would, in alchemy's terms, negate their efforts to free the spirit and soul from the body. A second possibility is that the *uniting* aspect of the first alchemical stage may already be influencing the participants, but the unconscious draws them toward each other in romantic love instead of joining spirit with soul. A sexual-romantic liaison then might be seen as a regression to the *massa confusa* preceding stage one, preventing this couple from reentering the alchemical therapeutic process together, thus leaving the former patient with the potentially destructive experience of a false start. If there was sexual contact without stopping the therapy, that offense could be understood as an alchemical travesty: acting as if the process is continuing while depriving it of the essential stage one separation from the body.

Reuniting *Unio Mentalis* with the Body

When the process has been faithful in pursuing stage one, its clear boundaries will have created the essential condition for the transforming integration of the opposites in the alchemists' second stage. As Jung describes it, in Dorn's second alchemical stage "spirit and soul [are] conjoined with the body" (1955, par. 664). It is extremely important to note, however, that this stage two integration is based on and requires clear stage one boundaries and is by no means simply a regression to "the *nigredo*, the chaos, the *massa confusa*" that preceded stage one's mind-body separation (ibid., par. 696). "Had they brought about this reanimation in a direct way," Jung cautioned, "the soul would simply have snapped back into its former bondage and everything would have been as before" (ibid., par. 742). Rather, Dorn wrote, "the body is compelled to resign itself to, and obey," the united soul and spirit. Elaborate procedures symbolize "the wondrous transformation . . . of body into spirit, and of [spirit] into body" (Gerard Dorn, in Jung 1955, par. 685). This is done alchemically by bringing forth "a certain heavenly substance hidden in the human body" (Dorn's words) which in reality is "the *imago Dei* imprinted in man" (Jung 1955, par. 681).

How might the patient's readiness to start moving into the integration, or *coniunctio*, of stage two be signaled? A particularly clear instance was of a patient who regularly expressed his gratitude that his current therapist, unlike his previous one, kept his personal life out of the work. Therapist and patient felt good about their especially clear boundaries, which were obviously important in this man's healing process. But there seemed to be a hint that his psyche was unconsciously reaching out when, around the time the therapist's marriage was breaking up—about which, of course, this patient consciously knew nothing—he asked to borrow a waiting room magazine because he had been struck by a poem in it which described a man and a woman joining and separating throughout their anguished divorce.

A little later, in an event which appeared outwardly like a nearly impossible coincidence, a coworker of the patient happened to show him a brief listing on which appeared the therapist's divorce filing, which had just taken place. Therapist and patient were both struck by the synchronistic meaning of that revelation. The work that followed did in fact demonstrate the readiness and need within the patient to start letting into his psyche some of the embodied reality of who the therapist was.

When the patient's psyche shows, in clear or subtle ways, a readiness to begin moving into the mysteries of stage two integration, what symbolic forms might arise possibly reflecting Dorn's "heavenly substance hidden in the human body"? For one patient, who had suffered childhood incest and adolescent rape, psychological and physical intimacy did not mix, although she yearned for it. In therapy, her intense fear produced prolonged resistance to explorations that would connect feelings and body. Eventually there was, however, some gradual movement toward a beginning of stage two conjunction of *unio mentalis* and body, and in one session she was able to allow herself to express interest in how her therapist saw her "from a man's view." As they ended that session, her psyche seemed to produce an embodied symbol of the *coniunctio* that was uniquely right for her. Instead of immediately heading for the door, she turned toward the two large plants next to them, gently took a dead leaf off one, stood there for a moment caressing the leaves of both plants, and then, turning to go, told her therapist that he should "just touch them sometimes."

Healing symbols may thus emerge from the alchemical pull toward *coniunctio* of *unio mentalis* with body, but that same archetypal potential may also give rise to a *distorted* expression in the form of a *concrete* sexual-romantic conjunction, a process explored more fully by Schwartz-Salant (1984). The tragic consequences of sexual boundary violations across a number of professional-client relationships have been well described by Rutter (1989) and others. But in psychotherapy in particular, when readiness for stage two *coniunctio* instead fuels a sexual-romantic liaison, the injury may also include a uniquely destructive dimension. The concrete relationship may actually displace the symbolic, healing alchemical *coniunctio* and preempt the essential transformation of the archetypally based transference.

The alchemical stage one *separation* of body from spirit-soul requires abstinence from sexual contact in therapy. The "wondrous transformation" of stage two *coniunctio*, sometimes represented symbolically by images of sexual union, can be displaced and precluded if actual, concrete sexual contact occurs between the participants. Ancient theory thus matches our modern experience which necessitates clear professional standards prohibiting sexual transgression. However, our understanding of the *coniunctio* mysteries is far from complete, and as analytical psychologists it is most appropriate that we be open to looking at the sexual-romantic shadow in our explorations of this healing archetype.

A particularly confusing and distressing form of the sexual-romantic shadow presents itself when we hear of transgressions by senior analysts who have seemed to possess especially powerful healing abilities. Perhaps understanding these situations would inform us of ways that any therapist's ego may be overwhelmed by a potentially healing archetype, contributing to sexual-romantic misappropriation of what should remain in the symbolic realm. It is

said that we have other "shadow colleagues" who have successful-
ly established committed relationships with former patients.
Assuming that this is so, perhaps we could learn more about the
coniunctio mysteries if we had ways to hear about their experiences, including insights about what happened to the alchemical
vessel when their therapeutic relationships ended and when these
patients were transferred to new therapists.

Our search for answers to these unknowns may require
more openness to exploring and working with the split off and frequently scapegoated sexual-romantic shadow. However, although
we recognize that traces of gold may lie hidden in this shadow, no
therapist today, with what we now know, can ethically rationalize
acting out with an intuition or feeling that "in this case it's really
love," any more than a sane person plays Russian roulette based
on an intuition that the gun won't go off this time.

Joining with the *Unus Mundus*

For Jung, "the crux of individuation" was the paradoxical integration of opposites in stage two (Jung 1955, par. 680). But beyond
that, the alchemists envisioned in a third stage the conjunction of
that whole individual with the *unus mundus*, which Jung
described metaphorically as "the potential world of the first day of
creation, when nothing was yet 'in actu'" (ibid., par. 760). This
imagery brings to mind a union with the oneness of the archetypal
Self, an ultimate psychological possibility sometimes symbolized in
the transference.

When such a potential *coniunctio* with the *unus mundus*,
or Self, is glimpsed through the transference, sexual-romantic
union may be incomparably alluring, and immeasurably damaging.
Sexual acting out between clergy and parishioners may sometimes
share a similar dynamic: clergy can be invested with the projection
of the Godhead, much as the psychotherapist might stand for the
Self through transference projections. The responsibility to parish-
ioner or patient is the same: to facilitate transformation of the projection into a living, embodied relationship with God or Self.
Sacrificing the transformative potential of the *unus mundus coniunctio* may be the unholiest of professional ethical violations.

In our analytic practices, the ultimate *coniunctio* of the

alchemists' stage three can stand as an inspiration as we strive to achieve and maintain stage one boundaries and, from that secure position, to work toward the mystery of stage two individuation through the integration of the opposites, opening always toward the stage three numinous *coniunctio* with the *unus mundus*, or with the Self. This alchemical model can help us be aware of some archetypal reasons behind our clear prohibition against mixing therapy with sex and can help us relate to that sexual-romantic shadow with the right mixture of judgment, humility, and compassion, as we continue to explore the mysteries of the healing *coniunctio*, shadow and all.

References

Jung, C. G. 1955. *Mysterium coniunctionis.* In *Collected Works*, vol. 14. Princeton, N.J.: Princeton University Press, 1970.

Rutter, P. 1989. *Sex in the Forbidden Zone.* Los Angeles: Jeremy P. Tarcher.

Schwartz-Salant, N. 1984. Archetypal factors underlying sexual acting-out in the transference/countertransference process. In *Transference/Countertransference*. Wilmette, Ill.: Chiron Publications, pp. 1–30.

John Steinhelber, Ph.D., is a clinical psychologist and Jungian analyst in San Francisco, California. He is a member of the C. G. Jung Institute of San Francisco, where he recently completed several years of participation, including chairmanship, on the Ethics and Grievance Committee. He is also a clinical faculty member in the Department of Psychiatry at the University of California, San Francisco, and for eight years served as their Director of Training in Clinical Psychology.

SELF SERVICE

Ann Belford Ulanov

The play on words in this title points to the ethical issues we face in analysis. At one extreme lies the use of others to serve our own needs. At some unconscious level, we treat them like a gas tank, there to service us, to give energy to our self. At the other extreme lies service to something beyond us, to the Self, to a meaning which gathers and constructs itself as we find and create it, which we find ourselves experiencing in a devotional way. No analyst, unless suffering from severe sociopathy or dissociation, sets out to do violence to an analysand, but some fall into it through entanglements of complexes which distort perception and thought. Despite the pertinence of R. C. Zaehner's pithy reminder about the wickedness of evil (1981, p. 27), the problem can be seen as equally large on the opposite side when we remember that "even the very disease takes on a numinous character" (Jung 1973, p. 377), and that for analysts, as Winnicott says, wickedness is illness (Winnicott 1963, p. 103). It needs to be treated, not simply condemned.

We know enough now about the danger of acting out transference and countertransference into physical exchanges between analyst and analysand, and about the equal and opposite danger of talking to death the hot feelings that pass back and forth between the two (Ulanov 1979, pp. 101-104, 109; 1982, pp. 77-78). The intensity, we know, can arouse hate as well as love, rage as well as tender rescue. Indeed, such archetypes can galvanize many outsized figures or emotions. The fact is that we need our complexes to play their proper role in order to sustain the arduous work of analysis. But if we work only within our personal complex, trouble must come, if not from imposing our own issues onto the analysand's, then from remaining locked into the personal levels of the material. Then the treatment will peter out, because the personal level is finite and gets exhausted; it simply is not enough. To move to the Self level in analysis is to raise issues of life-and-death importance that push us through our personal complexes to their underlying archetypal depths, as we respond to a particular analysand's reality.

Are there alternatives to acting out and to repressing or rationalizing a tremendously strong archetypal constellation? What can we do when the emotions stirred involve the strongest and most tempting of the constellations, sexual love? In it lie the treasures of *coniunctio*—a uniting of opposites as strong as love and hate deep inside us, between us, and in the world, too, so that we feel we are contributing to a greater good, not just succumbing to quick individual gratification. Sexuality is peculiarly suited to carrying almost all levels of psychic life, from a child's dependence to an adult's profound spiritual longings. Its preverbal, body-based, emotion-laden language of image, affect, and instinct makes it well suited to conveying our longings for union with split-off parts of ourselves, with a soulmate found in another, even with the transcendent. The intensity of our desire thus carried in body, heart, and soul recalls something as directly religious as the first commandment given by Yahweh to Israel and often repeated by Jesus: to love God with all our heart, mind, soul, and strength. When an erotic sexual archetypal constellation occurs in the transference and countertransference, analyst and analysand find themselves in the most flammable of situations. The fear of such intensity can drive both into sterile denial and rationalization.

Recent work on the primacy of the intersubjective field (Stolorow, Brandschaft and Atwood 1987) and on the necessity of imaginal seeing in order to avoid mechanically rendering the original organic wholeness into projection and counter-projection in which both analysand and analyst are held (Schwartz-Salant 1989) shows us how the dangers of ignition or denial increase if we equate the field with the Self. If the intersubjective field becomes idolized, we quickly forget the necessary limits of the analytic relationship. It is not, after all, one between equals. The hiring and the payment, "for services rendered," is a permanent component of the relationship, such that even as the two concentrate on the field between them, one is more responsible for what happens than the other. An analysand's dependence underscores this responsibility. Sexual feelings in analysis make a person especially vulnerable, not only because its language carries our heart and soul along with our instincts into communication, but also because sexuality brings us as close as we come in bodily terms in adulthood to that fullness of presence that we knew as infants with our parents. In such moments of intense sexual feeling, we cast off our defenses. Our capacity to be hurt is greatly enhanced, and we depend on the analyst to protect us (Winnicott 1963, pp. 249–250).

The feminine tendencies to relate by being-in-the-midst-of, being-one-with, taking the downward-going-road, lend themselves to working with skill and comfort within the intersubjective field (Ulanov 1971, pp. 169–179; 1981, pp. 76–80). But who is responsible for holding the situation? I say that the analyst is responsible. Guidance does not come from the field, nor from the analyst, but from the Self, which acts through the field and through the persons, and which all parties must listen to, but especially the analyst. That greater acuity which an analyst should have developed is what the analysand is paying for. If we make the field the Self, then the analytic couple assumes primacy over the real life of both analyst and analysand and also over the ego-Self couple that is growing in the analysand (Ulanov 1992a, p. 52). That assertion of power is a major betrayal of the analytical process, for the analyst then is not available to the analysand to inculcate a sense for living a real life.

The alternative of working with the erotic sexual field without either acting it out or denying it or rationalizing it into the Self lies, I believe, in both parties putting themselves under the authority of the Self and following its lead. This means sacrifices for both analyst and analysand, but, in unforeseen ways, thriving, too. Happily, the two meanings of my title meet: service to the Self turns out to answer our most particular personal needs as well as those of a commonality beyond us. We are thus reassured at a deep unspoken level that devotion to the transpersonal moves through and fulfills the personal. The two are not split. Rather, one orders the other (Ulanov 1971, p. 341).

Sacrifice sounds a familiar note that both analysand and analyst can recognize, for each knows that the limits of analysis make impossible their involvement with each other outside analytical sessions. When the analysis goes deep into early and painful wounds and explores fearful places where madness threatens, the borderline enactments of the anima or animus figure emerge. They stand with a foot on either side of the borders between ego and archetype, reasonableness and passion, sanity and madness. They bring with them gusts of archetypal emotion as they put their finger on the precise spots of ego vulnerability. The danger looms of being emotionally overwhelmed. One man, for instance, speaks about his attraction to his analyst and says he wants to carry her off to another country. He feels the burden of the one-way street of analysis, where the analysand must tell all the stories, reveal all the secrets, speak all the feelings, while the analyst remains comparatively unknown. This man knows the courage it takes to make something out of this asymmetrical relationship. But he suffers the sacrifice of a felt sense of dignity as he goes on revealing his secrets without a comparable return from the analyst. He feels he is sacrificing his natural urge to live out his attraction. He comes to see, however, that the momentum to go on making himself vulnerable springs from something beyond the analysis, from what he really loves and desires. He takes what bubbles up in the consulting room and lets its currents flow into his day-to-day living.

When a person lacks relationship to others in life outside the analysis, such sacrifice becomes harder, the analytical situation much more tense. Reality seems to flourish only within the analytical relationship. The urgency to live it right there becomes more compelling, and the sense of vulnerability all the more risky. Hidden in the urge for sexual gratification is purpose: the energy is going somewhere, and we must bend our will to the task of discovering just where and why. Sometimes the person finds the climate of desire too hot to handle and breaks off treatment. This is almost as hard for the analyst to bear as for the analysand, to see the work suddenly chopped off in mid-life. Sometimes, happily, the person comes back to pick up the work or at least to find better closure (Ulanov 1992b).

Sometimes an analysand sets out at some level of consciousness to snare an analyst into an affair. I have come to understand this as a move of desperation where the person feels that only power can secure the split-off parts of self so ardently sought (Ulanov 1979, p. 104). Often mixed into this power play lies a wish to defeat the analyst, even to wreck his or her career. It is for the analysand as if the sacrifice is reified and projectively identified with the analyst, so that only the analyst has to pay the price.

On the analyst's side there is a matching vulnerability. It is not the same as the vulnerability of transference love, but it is related. The analyst very much wants the analysand to take into her or his life what is created in the analysis. This feels like a kind of love for the analysand in which the analyst is made use of quickly enough and left behind. This is what countertransference love often becomes on the objective level. On the subjective level, an odd dialogue may occur between the complexes and wounds personified in the anima and animus figures of each person. Damaged or in good shape, the archetypal anima-animus couple will mirror and be mirrored by the analyst-analysand couple that forms and dissolves and forms again around the soul's desire to reach the center and heal the past. Analysis becomes a paradoxical exchange that is at once full-bodied and chaste, emotional and yet held within the limits of analysis. Each person addressed by the Self must face a tremendous energy suddenly let loose. When the male analysand discussed above, for example, was working on his feelings for me, I dreamed of a tiger, powerful, lustrous in its fur, and demanding that I drive it around the driveway of my house. With great exertion and concentration, I managed to do it.

Both analyst and analysand know that their feelings for each other can be lived symbolically but not literally either inside or outside the sessions. The thriving offered each person consists precisely in what flows into each of them from encounters in an intense erotic intrasubjective field, to be lived in their own separate ways. We must understand that when we confront an anima or animus issue, it sets off reactions on two levels: an ego level, where we are faced with a precise problem to struggle with, and an archetypal level, where we are ushered into the energies of the Self which demand to be realized and lived.

This last, this deep level of Self living, when really engaged, will rearrange all other aspects of personality, of object relations, of our life in the world. At the ego level, we are handed specific tasks to solve. At the shadow level, we are directed not just to go on uncovering shadow bits we would rather bury, but, perhaps surprisingly, to get at them by recollecting and claiming the good that already belongs to us (Ulanov 1993). We must remember what we love in order to reach what we hate. We must claim what we construct in order to tackle destructive elements (Winnicott, 1960). Finally, our anima-animus personifications transmute into bridges to lead us into Self territory. New objects come into being. We feel generating in us the beginnings of ideas, new ways of feeling, insights that fuel new belief in what matters. We are bound to be deeply moved by how much is given.

All of this work asks an energy sustained by a complex set of devotions. Hence the thought behind my title—that ethical issues ultimately resolve into service to the Self. Two examples must suffice. In the first, a supervisee, a male analyst, says that a woman analysand speaking of her love for him has accused him of denying the fact that he really is in love with her. "I'm not in love with her," he says, "but then I wonder." He felt hypnotized. What struck him with great force was this woman's "feminine courage" not to hide her vulnerable love for him and not to accept his denial without challenge. But did he too easily lose his own boundaries and merge his with hers? Still, in that part of him that could be so open to another he experienced "joy," pulled into union. Was this infantile striving to return to the womb, he asked, some comforting illusion to withstand the harsh reality of an ultimate loneliness? Listening, I heard what he said as the anima speaking, showing his basic orientation to reality, and his conflict about it. He felt an urge to live in kinship but also felt contempt for that urge. "You look down on this urge to union," I told him, "and then feel it persecutes you by tempting you into trouble." This remark triggered memories of his mother who had never had the centering courage he found in his analysand but always seemed to fall apart at the center, always wept and collapsed when she and his father disagreed and fought. He felt his mother was not reliably there for him because she could not reliably be present to herself.

In contrast, there stood his analysand, fragile like his mother but able to hold and center herself and speak out to the man upon whom she felt dependent, willing to expose her feelings and challenge him. She was, in psychoanalytic jargon, a woman who possessed her own penis. She had her animus within her, as part of her being. He felt hypnotized because she had touched a wound in his anima. When he saw this and really knew it, he could see and not despise his own urge to union and find his way to respond to his analysand along different lines. He could support her, ally with her ego in attempting to penetrate him with her own phallic thrust. His drive toward union with his analysand was in part an urge to go back and do it all over again, correctly, with his mother, and in part the result of a lavish admiration for what she, the analysand, had accomplished in herself. At this moment, in the work of this analytical couple, a piece of his wound in effect repaired itself as he allowed himself to feel the impact of his analysand's loving center and what it led him to find in himself. He was then able to aid her in sustaining herself in her own newfound strength to speak from that center and to be more of the woman she was meant to be. It was a moving exchange of feeling and understanding that arose through discussion of an ethical issue, all of it made possible because of open service to the Self.

The second example turns around an experience that is often deeply puzzling to analysts wherein the impersonal suddenly becomes personal when the countertransference endures, despite all our efforts to work it through (Ulanov 1982, p. 81). Although we know that our personal reaction is really not personal to us, we still feel it. It lives as if dissociated from the rest of our reality. In that way, it mirrors a dissociation in our analysand, which we know at first only hypothetically, although we are sure we must live with it, sometimes for months and months, as if it were a reaction drawn from the center of our person, even though we know very well it is not. Most ethical violations, I believe, come from such a situation, heightened when wounds in the analyst are touched. Then the analyst feels the pain and the contradiction intensely and cannot clearly mark out what belongs to whom, believing that what addresses the analyst also addresses the analysand and that the two of them are held in a gripping field that transcends both. It would seem a failure of nerve and faith to refuse to experience it, and it feels all but impossible to differentiate the induced reaction from the analyst's own feelings. It is then that we should consult a colleague. The frequent failure to do so touches the shadow side of Jungian analysis, I believe, and perhaps a weakness in all schools of depth psychology. We fear incomprehension and judgment and do not count on professional kinship. We do not trust what the great field of archetypal energy and of feeling might yield to a particular treatment or to general analytical understanding.

In this last example, an erotic tinge characterized the transference-countertransference field for a long part of a long analysis and then, amazingly, disappeared completely, as if folded into the integrated textures of analytical intimacy. It was as if the erotic factor was a separate ingredient, always before us, for months, but not really part of the analysand's personal life or my own. We spoke of it from time to time, and I used it to show the analysand how he found himself positioned with that eroticism toward others, even when it did not seem to yield much as a result of these efforts. Looking back, I now see that each effort was in fact part of a process that finally had an integrating resolution. We participate in our analysands' lives while not living at all with them outside our sessions. But still, we do live a history with each person that must affect and change each of us, analyst as well as analysand.

The alternative to repressing or acting out an erotic field lies, I think, in orienting the analysis around one summarizing question: What is the Self engineering? This orientation alone, in my experience, is strong enough and has enough of its own passion to contain erotic transference or countertransference and to allow its energies to support research into the ways we allow ourselves, analysts and analysands, to be used as servants of the process of living toward the Self. Because the Self is not a monolithic content that drops stonelike into the treatment, to work under its authority means we discover, create, and call the Self into being by strong ego efforts of inquiry and passionate interest in Self life and purpose. If such an erotic field blazes, it is to forge a uniting of ego and Self. For the analysand, an analysis fueled by an erotic field means a large overhauling of the personality, rather than simply reparative focus on one aspect of one's person. When anima or animus shapes a major part of the transference, a person's whole orientation to being will be called into question. Such will effect changes on every level of the analysand's life.

This was so in a case of an artistic man in his forties who dreamed that his anima ideal, a "goddess possessed of angel air," as he described her, was handed over to him by her husband who personified for the analysand the most crude and brutish aspects of his own shadow (see also Ulanov 1993). Following that dream encounter, he dreamed of his own father as needing the loving care he, his son, could provide, rather than as the judge who had always defeated his son's self-confidence by his severe judgments. At that point, he risked writing out his most intense and most oft repeated sexual fantasy and, in showing it to me, transferred onto me the self-loathing that accompanied it. He was then, inevitably, enraged at me, expecting that I would condemn him for that raw transference. But the dreaming went on its crusading way. He dreamed next of being captured and set to an ordeal of religious testing by four men of a different religious faith. When he accused them of going against their god, one of the men offered to take the sins of the other three onto himself. The dreamer then thought of Jesus, who had taken on the sins of others and reached to put his hand in Christ's as he faced the promised ordeal.

Now the purpose of the erotic tinge in the field between us became clear. I was carrying the hyphen, so to speak, between the dissociated elements in the analysand, between a ruthless aggressiveness expressed sexually—what he called "impersonal archetypal sex" that just gripped him and all who participated with him, while quite ignoring everything about their persons—and his genuine concern both for himself and for others. He needed the ruthless aggression, especially to throw off the condemning father voice, and in fact he did live the human personal dimensions of his life with much kindness and generosity to others. I carried the connection between these separated elements because I did not echo his condemnation of the sexual fantasy but rather endorsed its positive energies and excitement. Nor did I turn away from or rationalize the eroticism in the field, even though its dissociated elements might seem to conflict with the reality of my own commitment to those I love. I just held it in its appropriate place and bore the strain it brought. My role was to prepare the way for the experience of connecting up ruthless aggression with a genuine "capacity for concern" (Winnicott 1963). The analytical field held both aggression and concern, and the analysand could then finally integrate the two. Our analytical relationship connected the two halves. Then, at the point of integration, the erotic tinge simply fell away, its purpose accomplished.

What then followed was what the earlier dream had called "facing the ordeal." This turned out to be a reordering of every level of the analysand's being. On the ego level, specific tasks faced him, to be worked through with specific women in his life. On the shadow level, a wonderful dream image showed the chthonic energy now available to him in the figure of an enormous bull with flamingos on its head which he could summon by dancing a little jig. Cantering over, the bull would stop on his side of the line between them, ready to heed the man, who did not yet know where to direct this energy suddenly at his disposal. To him this image was raw aggression and sex, yet somehow connected through the birds to spirit. The shadow tasks unfolded gradually, involving him in differentiating himself from mother and father voices that still exerted powerful control over him and in facing his own eagerness just to escape, to veer off from any confrontation. At the anima level, he engaged both his beliefs about life, issuing in a formal commitment to the church, a step he had long considered, and open acknowledgment of his despair about an inner emptiness, laziness, and suicidal depression he found in himself. The energy to sustain all this work, which I understood as living toward the Self, as service to its advent and acceptance of it as life's center, came from the transformed erotic field. He was taking up the opus of *coniunctio*, unifying the disparate parts of his being, uniting with others in his life, and creating and finding his own path to the transcendent.

To serve the Self's advent, something very specific is required from the analyst, well beyond simply remaining in the field, erotic or whatever, until its purpose comes clear. What is also demanded is belief in the reality of the symbol, knowing that the psyche really does exist and that we serve its reality. The symbol is not a formula laid over something. It is not a "this" standing for a "that," but both a this *and* a that dwelling in the analytic moment. Archetypes are basic forms of being which once created go on forever (Lampert 1944). We cannot accept the reality of the moment when these symbols appear if we do not accept the being that the symbols configure. Being in all its reality should be embodied to begin with in the analyst's belief; the analyst's work confirms its reality, enabling the analysand to see it also, to recover the analytical moment as itself a symbol. It is that belief and confirmation which draw analysts to lives of open service to being.

This is the ontological premise of analytical method. The service of analysis to being is the grand alternative to the negative processes involved in either acting out or denying the erotic field which analysis so often enters. We are in the field, clearly, unmistakably, and ethically, accepting what is there, its consequences, its openings to truth, facing it with attitudes of directness. This is real; this is reality (Jung 1955, par. 754). We are not outside it, appreciating the experience esthetically but not really believing in it, thinking we can take it and then leave it. In the elements of belief, in entering into the reality of the archetype from which symbol and field arise, the healing processes of our work are made available to us and to our analysands. The reality itself achieves this great end, not the analyst, not the analysand, not the field. But to accomplish this end we must believe in its reality and live in it with all the necessary disciplines the belief brings with it.

Believing this way, as against acting out, means knowing reality as a constant presence and knowing that it knows us. The emphasis is on this *it*, on it relating to us, on how we relate to it, and how in time the analysand comes to relate to it. The intensity that first shows itself in an erotic field is released into these many relations to psychic reality. What the erotic tinge offers the analyst is penetration to psychic reality. That is where the passion is destined to go and finally arrives, where sacrifice becomes thriving at the deepest levels of life. For, like our images of heaven, each of us receives exactly what we need in our own idiosyncratic being. There can be found all the room that is needed for the intensity of reality to communicate itself and do its uniting work. Igniting or rationalizing the erotic field is a destructive and altogether unnecessary detour from the path of service to this reality whose flame of Self communication never goes out.

References

Jung, C. G. 1955. *Mysterium Coniunctionis*. *CW*, vol. 14. Princeton, N.J.: Princeton University Press, 1963.

Jung, C. G. 1973. *Letters*, vol. 1. Princeton, N.J.: Princeton University Press.

Lampert, E. 1944. *The Divine Realm: Towards a Theology of the Sacraments*. London: Faber and Faber.

Schwartz-Salant, N. 1989. *The Borderline Personality: Vision and Healing*. Wilmette, Ill.: Chiron Publications.

Stolorow, R. D., Brandschaft, B., and Atwood, G. E. 1987. *Psychoanalytic Treatment: An Intersubjective Approach*. Hillsdale, N.J.: The Analytic Press.

Ulanov, A. B. 1971. *The Feminine in Christian Theology and in Jungian Psychology*. Evanston, Ill.: Northwestern University Press.

_____. 1979. Follow-up treatment in cases of patient/therapist sex. *Journal of the American Academy of Psychoanalysis* 7(1):101–110.

_____. 1981. *Receiving Woman: Studies in the Psychology and Theology of the Feminine*. Louisville: Westminster.

_____. 1982. Transference and Countertransference. *Jungian Analysis*, M. Stein, ed. LaSalle, Ill.: Open Court.

_____. 1992a. Disguises of the anima. *Gender and Soul in Psychotherapy*, N. Schwartz Salant and M. Stein, eds. Wilmette, Ill.: Chiron Publications.

_____. 1992b. The perverse and the transcendent. *The Transcendent Function: Individual and Collective Aspects. Chicago 1992: Proceedings of the 12th International Congress for Analytical Psychology*, M. Mattoon, ed. Einsiedeln, Switzerland: Daimon Verlag, 1993.

_____. 1993. Spiritual aspects of clinical work. *Jungian Analysis*, vol. 2, M. Stein, ed. LaSalle, Ill.: Open Court, 1994.

Winnicott, D. W. 1960. Aggression, Guilt, and Reparation. *Deprivation and Delinquency*. eds. C. Winnicott, R. Shepherd, M. Davis. London: Tavistock, 1984.

_____. 1963. *Maturational Processes and the Facilitating Environment*. New York: International Universities Press, 1965.

Zaehner, R. C. 1981. *The City Within the Heart*. New York: Crossroad.

Ann Belford Ulanov, *Ph.D., is a Jungian analyst in private practice in New York City, a faculty member and supervising analyst for the C. G. Jung Institute of New York City, and the Christiane Brooks Johnson Professor of Psychiatry and Religion at Union Theological Seminary. With her husband, Barry Ulanov, she is the author of* Transforming Sexuality: The Archetypal World of Anima and Animus; The Witch and the Clown; Religion and the Unconscious; Cinderella and Her Sisters: The Envied and the Envying; *and her own forthcoming book* The Functioning Transcendent.

INDEX